Second Chances

THE U.S. CONSTITUTION

Jeffrey Ellner

Marci Brockmann International

Second Chances © 2022 Jeffrey Ellner
Ghostwritten by April Tribe Giauque
Edited by Marci Brockmann

Marci Brockmann
International

Printed in the United States of America
Published by Marci Brockmann International
21 Pulaski Road, Suite 152, Kings Park, New York 11754

Paperback: ISBN: 979-8-9867904-0-4
Hardcover: ISBN: 979-8-9867904-2-8
Kindle E-book: ISBN: 979-8-9867904-1-1
EPUB eBook – ISBN: 979-8-9867904-3-5
Library of Congress Control Number: 2022915897

SECOND CHANCES

Endorsements

Second Chances is an engaging primer on the creation of the Constitution—a scholar's assessment of the creation of this country's foundational document and the degree to which it helped to form and US. . Jeffrey Ellner breaks down what can be an intimidating document to frame a discussion about how well it establishes and protects freedom for all people. – George Miller, Social Studies Educator

As a woman of color, I find hope in this book because of its potential to disrupt the patterns and relationships that emerged from long-standing colonial principles and beliefs. Second Chances is an essential tool for authentic dialogue and action in establishing great equity among all American citizens. – Charmaine Roberts

Dedication

To my sweetheart, Ellen. Thank you for listening to my stories over the years and always believing that I could do it.

To my daughters, sons-in-law, and grandchildren, thank you for always being there and sharing your love with me.

My life is eternally enriched because of all of you.

Quotes

"Intelligence plus character is the goal of a true education." – Martin Luther King, Jr.

"Truth is like the sun. You can shut it out for a time, but it ain't going away." – Elvis Presley.

"Wyoming school children should not be required to stay the pledge of allegiance since the word 'indivisible' suggests that states cannot secede from the union." – A Wyoming Convention Delegate 2022.

"However difficult life may seem, there is always something you can do and succeed at." - Stephen Hawking.

"Success doesn't come from what you occasionally do; it comes from what you constantly do." – Marie Forleo.

"Educating the mind without educating the heart is no education at all." – Aristotle.

Contents

Foreward

"We don't fight the fights that we can win. We fight the fights that need fighting." – Sorkin, A., *The American President*, 1995.

What I've seen in the last six years (or more) has changed my opinion of the United States, and I'm now angry, disillusioned, and disappointed. Let me be clear. There is so much joy, love, beauty, kindness, caring, empathy, and compassion in this country and our world. Still, there is also hatred, stupidity, judgment, closed-mindedness, anger, frustration, resentment, violence, distrust, impudence, and fear that, lately, seems to be increasingly fueled by congressional representatives hell-bent on dividing us and instigating hatred, likely to distract us from their insidious profiteering, and power-hungry actions.

I'm a white, Jewish woman, a progressive Democrat, and a free-thinking contributor to ACLU, and the Southern Poverty Law Center, who believes that the content of one's character is the most important thing about a person. We are all the same. We all bleed the same. We all cry the same. We all love the same. We all want to live a safe, peaceful life filled with love, community, and the opportunity to provide for ourselves and our children. Globally, all of humanity wants the same things. I believe the majority of people who walk this earth are in agreement. We are all the same. Where did this country go wrong?

Secon♦ Chances, the book in your hands, traces the roots of humanity and the ways we live in community, from the earliest civilizations through the Imperialism and Colonization perpetuated by European monarchs, through the slave trade, the birth of the United States, the Founding Fathers' creation of our Constitution as a government for the people, and forward to our

1

modern era. Jeffrey Ellner shares the truth about what happened, but even more importantly, he shares with us possible reasons why it all happened the way it did and why we are still not living up to our potential as a nation. We still have a long way to go.

After enduring centuries of systemic, institutionalized racism, it has taken approximately 157 years, since the Emancipation Proclamation, to "progress" as far as we have, but whatever progress we have made is still hardly for all people. Throughout the 20th century, too many Black Americans and other people of color have suffered through the ubiquitous systemic racial inequality in economics and education. It is inescapable and affects every single decision, every day, for every Black person and person of color, in this country. And not just in the last two centuries, but even today.

The deaths of George Floyd, Breonna Taylor, Elijah McCain, Rayshard Brooks, Ahmaud Arber, Philando Castile, Michael Brown, Eric Garner, Alton Sterling, Oscar Grant, Freddie Gray, Bothan Jean, Atatiana Jefferson, Bettie Jones, Laquan McDonald, Tamir Rice, Dominique White, and too many others shake me to the core. They could be my students. They could be my neighbors, colleagues, or my children's friends. I look at all the young people I see, and I can't help but wonder who is next. As we continue to be divided by economics, race, religion, political party, and opinions on controversial issues, and while social justice is being hotly debated, I wonder how far it will go before things change.

As a mom, I think about all the millions of mothers of Black boys and men (and women and girls) who constantly fear the health, safety, and welfare of their amazing sons (and daughters). For them, it could be deadly to walk to the corner store or school, take a simple drive to visit grandma or travel a regular commute to work.

Too many innocent Blacks are stopped, questioned, harassed, pulled over, arrested, roughed up, sized up, ridiculed, suspected, scrutinized, accused, and killed for no other reason than the color of their skin. As Neil deGrasse Tyson wrote on Me*ium, in his article *Reflections on the Color of My Skin*, everyday Blacks face: "Hyper-focused unfair, biased scrutiny and false, dangerous accusations made by police against people of color whose only 'crimes' were: DWB (Driving While Black), WWB (Walking While Black), and of course, or JBB (Just Being Black)."

My best friend's Black husband has gotten pulled over, harassed, and questioned by the police for no other reason than being Black in his own Long Island, New York neighborhood dozens of times in the last couple of years. Every Black person I've talked to has these same experiences every day. This has continued as too many of us carry on with our lives and are busy with the millions of distractions that parade through our lives. Many turn a blind eye because they think it doesn't affect them, but it does.

> If one of us faces persecution, we all face persecution.
> If one of us faces injustice and cruelty, we all face injustice and cruelty.

I have faced a bit of antisemitism. As a child, I was spat on, tomatoes were thrown in my face, and last winter was insulted and told I'm not *really* white because I am a Jew—that I'm a *fake* white person. (As if being white was the epitome of personhood.) The vitriol with which this was stated scared me and temporarily caused me to shrink away and cower, but I had the luxury of hiding behind my pale skin and not dealing with it head-on. I closed my eyes to it and moved on. I have this luxury. I had my white privilege to hide behind. Too many of us hide here in plain sight—in doing so, we are part of the problem. Our silence perpetuates this awfulness.

I've tried explaining white privilege to people and it is frustrating when they don't see it. I see and feel and experience my white privilege—every damn day. I try to speak up and spread awareness and educate the ignorant while Black people get murdered for being Black—every damn day.

I can go jogging, ask for help after a car crash, listen to loud music in public, ask for directions, talk on my cellphone, sit on my front porch, go to a party, shop, read a book in my car, carry boxes of my stuff, run, take out my wallet, breathe, and live all without being harassed, bullied, beaten, questioned, or killed just because of the color of my skin. For every single one of these banal actions, Black people have been murdered. This is absurd.

Sure, it's technically illegal to discriminate against someone because of gender, skin color, sexual identity, or preference. Still, it happens daily and often by those who have sworn to protect and defend US citizens and our inalienable rights.

People have turned a blind eye or expressed their *thoughts and prayers* for too long and then moved on. For too long, this has continued.

When the tragic murder of George Floyd broke the news, the tightly coiled spring erupted. Across the nation, citizens with anti-racist passions took to the streets, the cities, the small towns, and Washington to make their collective voices heard. The first amendment of our Constitution protects our right to protest. It is ingrained in our citizenship that our responsibility is to challenge overreaching authority. "Congress shall make no law abridging the freedom of the press, or the right of the people peaceably to assemble, and to petition the government for a redress of grievances." – James Madison.

"America isn't easy. America is advanced citizenship. You want to claim this land as the land of the free? Then the symbol of your country cannot just be a flag. The symbol also has to be one of its citizens exercising his right to burn that flag in protest. Now show me that, defend that, celebrate that in your classrooms. Then you can stand up and sing about the land of the free."– Sorkin, A., The American President, 1995.

The most American thing we can do is protest to redress grievances. And yet, armed like they were going to war, the police forces in our nation, who are sworn to protect the citizens, opened fire on peaceful protesters with tear gas and rubber bullets and drove armored police cars through crowds mowing down innocent, peaceful protesters who were simply and peacefully protesting the pervasive, systemic racism in the US.

After being told that every method of peaceful protest is wrong and inappropriate, frustration took over. Yes, some were fed up with the lack of improvement on this huge issue and the magnitude of the lives lost. Some of all races looted and set fire to buildings to express their vehemence, frustration, and anger at the banal platitudes being offered. The police should have focused their attention on the looters and protected the peaceful protestors in their efforts to keep the peace and avoid draconian curfews. This leaves every one frustrated and disillusioned over and over again.

> "Things aren't fine. We have so many problems that we don't even want to look at them anymore. They just blend together in this great big noise, and pretty soon, we can't even hear ourselves think. That's not even the worst part. The worst part is that we feel like we can't do anything about it. That's a tragedy. Because we can...You don't really know how much you can do until you decide to stand up and try." – Dave, 1993.

In 2017, Education Week wrote there were 130,930 public and private schools in the United States with approximately 58.8 million students. In New York City alone, there are approximately 1 million students (Riser-Kositsky, 2019). What are we teaching them all? What facts, skills, strategies, and values are we teaching them? According to the education department of New York State, the "mission is to raise the knowledge, skill, and opportunity of all the people in New York. Our vision is to provide leadership for a system that yields the best-educated people in the world" (NYSED.gov., 2019). Are we doing that? Are we raising the knowledge, skill, and opportunity for ALL our students? Have we made it possible for all our students to receive an equitable education with the same access to technology, exemplary educators, curricula, and texts? Or have we allowed our fears and biases to infringe upon our children's rights to learn critical thinking skills so that they can learn not only those events that happened but why they happened so they can create a better, more equitable, and inclusive future?

We need to learn about history and the mistakes and atrocities humans heaped on each other, so we learn not to do those things again to prevent history from repeating itself. With each new generation, we must perpetuate that we can and should do better and be more inclusive, accepting, humanitarian, and noble. To accomplish this, we must teach the critical thinking it takes to be an active citizen and encourage the next generation to use the power of their voice – their votes – to create a country that represents our shared ideals and values and encourages our children to do better than we have done and make the country and our planet a safer, more peaceful, more loving and humanitarian place to live.

I am angry, frustrated, scared, and heartbroken. I don't have the answers, but there are actionable things we can do. We can support Black-owned businesses. We can donate money to the victim's families. We can educate ourselves and our children.

I don't pretend to know what it feels like, but I will forever stand with my BIPOC sisters, brothers, friends, students, and neighbors. The evil that is racism must stop. I commit to being part of the change that is long overdue in the world, to walk the talk every day as we take baby steps into a more equitable, peaceful, safer future with all our inalienable rights of life, liberty, and the pursuit of happiness. We all deserve a second chance.

–Marci Brockmann

Note To Reader

"Things that cannot be hidden for long - the sun, the moon, and the truth." – Unknown

The history published in books does not always tell the truth. Many people know this, yet many still tell you what they want you to believe.

Stop for a second and ask yourself: do the talking heads tell the actual truth or just their perception of the truth? Why do they want to convince you that they know best? Maybe they don't know that truth, or they don't want to tell you the truth. Shouldn't they just try to inform you of the truth?

This is a different kind of book. I will take you on a journey from the beginning of time to the origins of humans, the history of America, and why we are in such a mess today. This book is about change. I demonstrate how the earth has been through many different changes over millions and billions of years and that change is a part of our life and always will be part of our life.

The change I want to see deals with *America* and the concept of freedom we all think we believe in. I must tell you the truth about what has really happened over time, and I am committed to that endeavor, to tell the truth. That's why we must start at the beginning.

Who discovered America? Columbus? Native Americans? I will reveal the truth of the Native tribes who called themselves *The People* and helped begin the start of the history of America.

If we are focused on freedom and true freedom, we must look at the entire history and look deeply into our Constitution to see if we have not only been in it for ourselves from the beginning. Is there anything you can look forward to about this country or take pride in?

Our country started as a place for *Secon* *Chances,* but it has missed the mark and has not lived up to that ideal. We have seen how some aspects work, but many things have only been pretense.

The United States has accepted immigrants to this country, but something is missing. We honestly never treated them equally. These immigrants were never offered the same opportunities. The fabric of American history has been riddled with discrepancies. Hasn't this unfair treatment gone on long enough? It is time to try to bring this country and all its disparate parts together to make it all work. Thus, it is time for *Secon* *Chances.*

1

INTRODUCTION

"We did not come to fear the future; we came here to shape it." – Barack Obama

A democracy is a system of popular government through which *all eligible citizens* are entitled to participate. America was built with this foundation—the Constitution was the key focus. It sounds familiar, ideal, and yet simple. However, have you ever stopped to think about the significance of why you think this way? Is this something you just accept because you are an American?

Have you ever questioned the men who wrote the Declaration of Independence and the Constitution? Why were only fifty-five men in charge of setting up the country's foundation—in secret? Were women, enslaved people, or other minorities involved in creating the most excellent *Law in the Land*? Were their opinions even considered? Have you ever thought about asking questions like that? After all, the Constitution is the *Law of the Land*, and yet, wouldn't you like to understand why such a small few were able to create the law to which we are all subjected?

Think about all that you know or think you know about American history. You probably have heard about or studied stories about the Declaration of Independence, the Revolutionary War, The Articles of Confederation, and the Constitutional Convention. Well, buckle up. I will share the other half of those stories and the biased process involving only a limited number of men, no women, and no other diversity.

Ideally, according to the words in the Constitution, the citizens, or *We the People,* hold power. *We, the People,* can participate in the government through our elected representatives. *We, the People,* have the power to have a voice through our vote. What does it mean to have an elected official represent your viewpoint? Have we, as Americans, ever approached any kind of conversation about that concept?

The Constitution is ideal. It is uniquely American; however, why did only a few have the right to set it up in the first place without proper representation of all people—women, enslaved people, and other minorities? Why? Did the Founders think that any of these people had worth or could contribute something valuable to the document? In the 18th Century, was that the case?

The evidence that I will present will be challenging to you—and mind-blowing. This is now the 21st century, and we have a lot of work to do. However, we must attempt to have all of our voices represented together.

We must pursue, starting again, to create a Constitution that can be selected by *a majority of us* instead of a *few* Founding Fathers —we must choose a direction and pursue it. The Founders never considered all the people. How much time have we wasted living this way?

Perhaps we will hear a clarion call when most of us get together and point us in that direction. It won't be easy, but it must be started.

The preamble to our Declaration of Independence begins with the words:

> *We hold these truths to be self-evident, that all men are created equal, that they are endowed by their creator with certain inalienable rights, and that among these are life, liberty, and the pursuit of happiness.*

These were the goals in 1776.

The goals of the Constitution also appeared in its preamble. Those words were as follows:

> *We, the people of the United States of America, in order to form a more perfect union, establish justice, ensure domestic tranquility, provide for the common defense, promote the general welfare, and secure the blessings of liberty to ourselves and our posterity, do ordain and establish this constitution for the United States of America.*

The words are true. They are the ideals. But from the very beginning, the application of these words and this process were represented by only a few members of the economic elite, all of whom were white men. Therefore the words become platitudes. The next question is how those words in the Constitution have been pursued.

Now that I have asked *why* a *few* Founders were able to establish the paths to attain the rule of law for all of us, what do those words mean to us now? Why do we believe these words? What significance did these words have? What do they mean today? What do these ideals stand for? Perhaps they need to be rewritten to have more significance, so we can make them a reality —those words should represent all of us.

Let's go back to 1787 to the Philadelphia Convention and see how we got into the situation we are in today. Perhaps we can find a path to climb out of where we are and get work, and try to fulfill those ideals in our preamble.

To provide a perspective, few of our colonial residents even knew about our Declaration of Independence. In 1776, few of our colonists could read or write, and most didn't keep an ear out for declarations while the War of the Revolution was being fought. There were no newspapers, magazines, radio stations, or television stations. The only way to spread the news was to talk to each other, but because of the colonists' different languages and customs, many didn't speak to each other in this way. They were busy raising their children, working their farms, growing their small businesses, and trying to survive a war they had no control over!

The colonists who could understand believed these goals were attainable, but 240 years later, they still have not been fully attained. These goals were expressed as words, but they were mere words to be used as a rallying cry so that we could address the needs of our nation for the expanding war with England.

England was never our mother country for all those who escaped her grasp. We fought to get free from England. We did not obtain our freedom from England until we fought that war. We fought for that freedom, and we got ourselves free. But now what?

The words of our Declaration of Independence cannot and should *not* be rewritten. They hold truth, but the Constitution, which followed more than a decade later, is what I am questioning in this book. There are truths, but portions of it should be rewritten, with the majority voice having a more significant say in the words we put to paper to establish a new path to travel together.

If the Founding Fathers had considered what the words *We the People* meant, and they meant them to represent everyone— women, enslaved people, and other minorities, we wouldn't need the 13th, 14th, 15th, and 19th Amendments. Think of all the mess we could have avoided if they had done just that!

So today, we must start by asking questions, finding the answers, finding a path, putting it all together, and mustering the will to proceed. We must try to achieve what the majority of us want. We must prepare to fight again, but without weapons—this time, we need to fight with the truth.

What you learn in this book will urge you to ask questions. Still, we must consider the majority to see how these opinions can be blended so that we can *all* be represented and apply all of our voices to the revision of our Constitution.

In this book, I will share evidence as to why I believe the Constitution we live under is inadequate—I mean, after all, the few people who wrote it did not even think of the generations who would follow them. Some might argue that what they did has been *implie*✦ to include all of us, but actions speak louder than words. The actions of people become the truth. This is an idea I have been mulling over since I started writing down my thoughts in 1967—over fifty years ago. Did the Founders only write and state what they wrote so that they personally could benefit from what they were attempting to do? Was it all for their personal gain? Looking back at history, it certainly seems that way.

Now, the ideals of the Preamble had never made it into many of the minds of those who endorsed the document. There was bitter contention and division during the convention, and I will expose those truths in chapters 4-8. The Founders stated their reasons and withheld their signatures as well. The details of that convention, those who participated in its meetings, will be presented verbatim. These words are for your edification.

This book was written because *we* must start telling *our* history by sharing both sides of the story. In this way, we will find the truth. As we proceed, you'll learn why it is that way.

Now, no matter what, this is our story. All of us, good or bad, allowed it to happen, and we must consider our new choices and how we can work together until we have the majority who agree that this is another clarion call we must answer.

We have many decisions to make, and all of us should be invited to participate together in creating *our* new Constitution.

It is now time to share all this because the country into which I was born seems to be melting. We are no longer what I thought we were. The division is enormous, and it is tearing at the fabric of our nation. How did we get to this place? But more importantly, how can we turn it around?

We must take care of all of the human beings who populate our land and those who seek a better life to pursue their dreams. After all, that's what they came here for, to make those dreams come true. This is a pledge we make to our citizens and extend to those seeking citizenship in our nation.

Here is a great question. Can America become the *Beacon on a Hill* people have sought for centuries? I believe so.

Now, all people have the right to exist! At one time, we wanted those huddled masses, the courageous people born elsewhere who braved the journey to get here and hoped for the fulfillment of the promise of the ideal of America. It seems that their hopes had been dashed for more than 200 years. Isn't it time to fulfill the dreams of a majority of us?

How did we get to where we are today? It wasn't easy. As we consider and explain our history, there is still much more to think about; so much more to do. I don't believe each of us, even with our opinions, will find the path we all need to pursue and achieve our dreams without help. I present the other side of the truth and offer ideas, but we must read the signposts we see along the way and find a pathway forward to make things happen for all of us.

Perhaps we can turn this country around from the present to find a road where all of us can achieve our dreams: a nation where we feel secure and where we want the best for everyone and all of our offspring and where we can achieve it.

To make anything happen, people must be passionately involved in the goal set by everyone who participates in achieving that goal. This means *majority rule*, not the decisions made by a few that support that idea. Only a few of our forebears, a very few, made the decisions and the rules and enacted the Constitution that we live under today. The few who made the decisions and set the direction to travel were very small.

The concept of America was just an idea but did not fully come to pass. Why? Two primary reasons: 1) not everyone was able to participate in it. Sure, there was excitement and passion in it, but it had no force behind its ideas to make a better America than we had then or have now. And 2) Humans are not perfect. We never were and will never be, but together we can find a new path on which all of us can walk. We may do better when we're not limiting the number of people involved in taking that walk with us.

Only a very few of us set the foundations of this country's government and Constitution, but remember, hardly anyone else was invited to participate—at the time, some states did not even send representatives. You can see the unintended consequences of that event. Not even all fifty-five men at the convention voted to ratify the Constitution, and not everyone in attendance approved of what the convention decided should be in the new American Constitution. But that was their choice.

Now, *all* of us are invited to participate. By adding our opinions, all of us will be helping others to move forward with what we need to get done. Buckle up! It is going to be a bumpy ride. The path forward must be accessible to everyone, and we can try to make a difference. I believe that we have to do this together to accomplish anything significant.

I will start our story with the truth and stick to the plan. Our path has never been straight; however, we can all get to work if you are ready.

2

Education and Learning

You've got to be taught to hate and fear
You've got to be taught from year to year
It's got to be drummed in your dear little ear
You've got to be carefully taught
You've got to be taught to be afraid
Of people whose eyes are oddly made
And people whose skin is a diff'rent shade
You've got to be carefully taught
You've got to be taught before it's too late
Before you are 6 or 7 or 8
To hate all the people your relatives hate
You've got to be carefully taught

> —*You've Got to be Carefully Taught*, written by
> Richard Rodgers and Oscar Hammerstein
> from the Broadway play *South Pacific* in
> 1950.

If you think about the lyrics, they state that we are taught to hate, fear, be afraid, and become prejudiced and biased toward others (race, gender, ideas, thought, character, etc.). Education is the only means available to us to prevent the same things from repeating again and again with barely any changes from the past.

If schools are the fostering zone for this, shouldn't parents get involved and stay involved the whole time to help foster truth, facts, and thinking, other than learning about a bias?

Schools and educators have fostered this repetition for far too long. We must find the time to make our educational system better and more efficacious. Our work must offer the hope of improvement. It can prevent the constant repetition that has gone on long enough in this country and break into learning how to think for yourself, not just memorize facts and spit them back.

Education should ask the basic questions, provide a path to teach more, and give a direction to prepare better. What we teach currently is answering simple *what, who, where* or *when* questions. However, we must also create a basis for the long-term significance of these decisions and choices by asking *why* to get at the heart of where our collective values reside.

Why is the most critical question to ask!

Why is this concept significant? *Why* should teachers focus on this primarily? The answer to the *Why* question provides a path to the truth, unlike only asking who, what, when, and where. The response to the *why* question alone provides a path for thinking about our collective purpose, values, and future.

Learning is the process of applying lessons from our shared history and evaluating how our collective needs were either met or unmet, and then blazing a new path toward a more inclusive and compelling reality.

Plato said, "If a man neglects education, he walks lame to the end of his life." This is my attempt to help correct and heal the lameness you might have regarding the history of this country. If you think about the following statement from Plato's *Republic*, "The direction in which education starts a man, will determine his future in life," you might feel inclined to take a few steps in a different direction than you were previously headed. It's perfectly acceptable to make course corrections by a few degrees because, in the end, your course will be corrected toward more truth.

Not everything is always the truth. We should start anew. The truth comes to each of us independently. Plato also said, " No one is more hated than he who speaks the truth." I hope that you can keep your emotions in check while I present the truth that will be new to many of you. I take my challenge as your teacher through these lessons very seriously.

Each of us must learn from our teachers. Those teachers give us signposts and directions, but we may choose which path we want to proceed. Our teachers have to teach the curriculum, but students must learn more. They must learn to apply what those teachers teach them to lead their lives and dreams.

Teachers have huge responsibilities and, therefore, need to be paid more so that we can attract effective and intelligent teachers who are not afraid of asking tough questions.

When I started teaching in 1960, I was paid $5,000 a year! That was ridiculous. I was entrusted to instruct the malleable minds of young children, and I was limited in my earning potential because I only worked from September to June. I also had to work other jobs within the school, which required me to stay late. I had to work after school. Some days I missed dinners with my family. I needed those other jobs to make a living, provide for my family, and establish a lifestyle I wanted to maintain. From my experience, that is a fact. Teaching is noble and enjoyable. Teachers should be able to make a comfortable living because so much is demanded of them.

Education requires support, caring, and monitoring, and the community and parents must be involved. That is an integral part of education. Teachers work with people and need all of their skills to prepare for class. My question to you, readers, are teachers prepared for their classes?

From my experience, it seemed like the school board never believed that teachers had to prepare lesson plans, take attendance, give and grade exams, record grades, grade homework, etc. I don't know what they thought teachers did with their classes, but I was a great teacher and did all that I could to help foster thinking. In my time, few parents were ever concerned with all the demands teachers had to cope with in and out of the classroom. Do parents or school boards respect teachers and all that they do? It sure doesn't seem like it.

Now, teachers, if you are reading this book, I want to ask you a few questions. How many of you teach your students how to think? Do you teach them how to defend their positions on issues they are learning? I learned to think and teach in school from the readings historians wrote about Socrates. He was a teacher from early Greece who couldn't even see, but he could teach his students to reason.

His famous quote, "Education is the kindling of a flame, not the filling of a vessel." That is what I hope to do here. The ideas in this book are filled with heat and energy and could combust into a flame, lighting your mind on fire to new ways of thinking.

Socrates also said, "I cannot teach anybody anything. I can only make them think." With his words fresh on your mind, let's plunge into the next story.

As a teacher, I discovered that few of my fellow teachers cared what students thought. They were there just to fill a job, get a paycheck, and be on their way. I wonder if teachers are doing that today? Are they just lecturing? Or are they thinking about the students and how to shape their minds by asking *why?* We need youth to think by asking questions and pondering the answers, finding the truth for themselves, and following that.

In all the years I was privileged to teach, I challenged my students to think, ask why, and challenge their thoughts. I asked them questions. I asked for their opinions as to why they were speaking like that. I thought that my classes were always lively with questions and discussions.

Teachers teach their students to think. Good teaching allows your students to learn how to use their minds. After teachers talk, teach, and show and demonstrate, they need to test that knowledge to see if their students got it. I would measure my classes with this thought, "Was the lesson powerful and meaningful enough so that now students can apply it?"

There are parts of education where memorization works, especially in the natural sciences - chemistry, biology, and physics. Still, you can go on from there to think about what you have learned for yourself and make strides in your understanding.

Teachers have to follow a math and English syllabus, etc. You start that way; they are basics. After you accept that and achieve the goals of that syllabus, you can then learn to memorize, but you have the world ahead of you. We must consider the early lessons that we were taught. We were asked to memorize many of those lessons; we followed those instructions. However, students have the freedom to find the truth for themselves, and they also have to learn the rules of the road. These rules apply to each of us and might be different for each course you take.

Teachers, you will not regret doing this for your students; by adding critical thinking skills and evaluating everything you teach, you are getting your students ready to think independently. Learning how to think on their own is not a waste of time; it is critical for life!

Here is a lesson I learned and never forgot. In 8th grade, I had learned from teachers (facts and things to memorize), but I knew there was more to learning; I wanted to know *the WHY* for myself. This is not the same as when you're in math class, where you must memorize and memorize whatever you've been taught. I had to do it with baby steps.

I was in the eighth grade when I had to move and start attending a new school in October. The first test I was given in my new school was a social studies test. I learned the lesson at that time, but I didn't understand it from my teacher. I knew it from myself. I have kept those memories with me for my entire adult life.

Monday came, and I did what I was asked to do. My teacher gave us an assignment on a Friday to memorize the preamble to our American Constitution. We were to memorize it over the weekend and return on Monday to write it down in class without help. I wrote it out, but then I offered several thoughts about the preamble.

The teacher returned the test, and I saw that I had only obtained a C. I did what the exam asked me to do, but I wanted to add my opinion about the preamble. I wanted its expressed goals to be explained. However, the teacher did not want or ask for this. Therefore, I received a low grade.

If the teacher could not define those goals listed in the Constitution, *how coul‎ they ever be achieve‎?* I learned that my opinion was not to be added to his tests, but that never stopped me from thinking that way. I knew then and there that if I became a teacher, I would ask my students *why* questions to ensure learning had occurred.

Think about it. If the Founders didn't prod us to think, how could those goals in our preamble ever be achieved? People need to express their own opinions. I do, but how could others learn to appreciate what some words meant to each of us? If we can answer questions with our thoughts, we consider what must be done.

In my classes, over the years, I asked my students to provide their opinions and beliefs about what was being presented in class. I told them that just giving back what I said does not suggest learning. I wanted them to ask the question, *why?* I wanted to hear what the students thought was necessary about what we were discussing. I also wanted to hear about the opinions of their classmates' thoughts and answers.

I offered different ways that students could train themselves to think about thinking. This is called metacognition. With practice, students themselves can be made more aware of how they individually learn and how they can develop their understanding. They undoubtedly benefit from this instruction, especially when they are out of school and living independently.

When I asked a question in class that required some insight and end thinking, they all tried to answer by providing the answer to the questions of who or what. I asked them to respond by explaining *why* that happened that way. What made that event significant? How can we use that lesson going forward?

We can learn what happened with the facts, but why should we accept what happened in the past? What about that happens now? How do we join the past and the present and conceptualize what we need to do to make learning more beneficial and have that learning appreciated by all of us?

Sure, you know for yourself by listening and writing. Your thoughts on exams, especially on essay questions, help explain your thoughts, but do those exam questions allow you to modify your thoughts as we advance? But what should future generations learn from your efforts? What teaching methods are discussed so we can contextualize our thoughts and pass those thoughts to our children?

Teachers, when looking at history, it is vital to show both sides of the story so that students can learn from the mistakes others made and so they can help to improve their future. We have to do it through education. We have an opportunity right now to chart a new path of showing both sides of history. We don't need to teach the traditional and the slanted view. We can stop teaching hate and teach the truth.

I must share another teaching story. I was teaching in one high school and doing an excellent job for a decade, but I felt the need to expand my horizons, and when I got an opportunity, I took it. I was told about an opening in another high school. I went for an interview and was offered a two-year position as chairman of that high school's Social Studies Department.

What happened during that first year is significant. Under my direction, the teachers in that department and I agreed that we would create final exams for our students in groups. Those meetings were attended by all of the teachers in the department I inherited and by the two or three new teachers I had hired. We met quite a few times and prepared questions for the exams.

As chairman of the department, I was supposedly in charge. The day after those exams were ready to end mimeographed, I thought they were placed in the school's safe—protected. I had work to do as chairman during the rest of the day. I had two students who worked for me, one before lunch and one after. Both of these young women, who were not in my classes but in the classes of others in the department, each came to my office to perform the tasks they were directed to do.

I noticed they came into my office with all kinds of things written on their arms in ink. When I asked them what was on their arms, they told me they had been given the answers to the final exams to be administered the next day. They were given the means to cheat and were ready to provide the answers to other students! This would have given them an unfair advantage.

During my free time, I went to the administration and asked them if they had any advice on my next step. They said the next step was up to me; I was the chairman, and it was my decision.

I decided I had to act. I agreed that I would rewrite the exam. I used a copy of a different exam I had previously operated on from my previous school. That afternoon, I did not go home when school ended. I stayed through the night. I mimeographed enough copies of that exam so that we would have exams for the 400 students taking that final the next day.

I spent the entire night mimeographing, collating, stapling, and separating all those exams so that the scheduled final exam could be administered in the gymnasium the following morning. Honesty, secrecy, and an unbiased exam was my goal.

I had leveled the playing field. Everyone who had to take that exam could now start equally with everyone else. All the teachers who had encouraged their students to cheat were now caught off guard.

I still couldn't believe that teachers in my department would cheat, but they did what they did. During the exam, the teachers tried to pull a fast one, and my actions prevented that from happening.

During the administration of the updated exam, the teachers of my department complained to me. Still, I paid little attention to them and more to the students in my charge because I was in charge of administering the final exam. Those teachers complained to the administration, and I had to respond. I was asked to attend the meeting between the principals at the high school, and I did.

After they finished chiding me for what I had done, I offered my resignation effective at the end of the next school year. I only wanted to leave teaching on my terms, not anyone else's. This experience taught me that many teachers don't care. But I cared, and I'm glad I never backed down.

From my experience, teachers were required to be in school for one or more evenings throughout the school year to meet and speak with the parents of their students. Only a few parents were interested in doing that, but the teachers were required to be there! Why weren't these parents interested, or are many parents of these children derelict in supporting their child's education?

When their students didn't do their assignments, parents never cared. They didn't respond to phone calls when teachers called in the evening. They didn't find time to respond to notes teachers would send home. Perhaps they never got the messages that were sent. Why shouldn't teachers think that these parents cared? Parents expect the children's teachers to do it all.

I remember one situation when I wrote a letter to two parents that their son had not completed one single assignment for an entire year between September and June. I wrote to those parents, and neither of those parents ever responded to me. The student failed the class and had to attend summer school instead of football camp. The parents stormed into my classroom to complain, saying that it was my fault their son failed and that I should pass him! What about their behavior throughout the year would make me think they cared?

Parents, I implore you to participate in your children's education or accept some of the responsibility and not blame it on the teacher. We can all work together to be better prepared and honestly try to make teaching more than a job and one of engaging youth in learning about how to think.

Teachers, remember to help your students think and reason by asking the questions of *why*. Don't dumb down the educational system by not encouraging your students to ask the question of *why*. America, come on! You can rise to a higher level. You have the tools to do that. Now, the question is, do we have the will to do that?

> When statistics rank America as falling behind in education, it is heartbreaking. According to a recent column by Nicholas Kristof, "America was rated 10 out of 64 compared to what other countries are achieving with their economies, and the World Bank ranked America 35th out of 174. 'Our greatest vulnerability is not what other countries do to us but what we have done to ourselves.' The United States cannot achieve its potential when so many Americans fall short of theirs."

When studies say that a fifteen-year-old can't read at a level expected of a ten-year-old, there is something wrong. Teachers, teach your students, care for them, and the future will be bright again.

America's future is more dependent on the fact that we must educate our youth, yet we are underperforming, and we are not achieving most of the goals of what our schools have been set up to do.

Jefferson said, "To penetrate and dissipate these clouds of darkness, the general mind must be strengthened by education." If we take the quote's words to heart, teachers, parents, students, and all of America, reclaim your education. Read, ask questions, attend, and take responsibility to learn and educate yourself. You are doing that here with the book *Secon♦ Chances*, and I thank you for that.

Why is it true that many more of us believe that the American dream will not be fulfilled? We must return to the lyrics from the beginning, "You've Got to be Taught." Teachers, what are you teaching? We must teach our youth to think and engage. Teachers, if you are ready, please be willing to do the hard work of enlightening our students. America, we have to get to work to save our youth.

3

Earth and Prehistory

"Everything started as nothing."
– Ben Weissenstein.

"Changing is nature's true law."
– Unknown.

Earth formed approximately 4.5 billion years ago. Life began upon the rocks and layers. There was no atmosphere to support life. As volcanic heat and gasses were released, water vapor was trapped by billions of particles of earth, and slowly over millions of years, an atmosphere appeared.

A geologist can tell by samples found in rocks from around 2.4 to 2.1 billion years ago that the earth was interspersed with glaciers and ice as the change cycle began. Planet Earth started a cycle of heating and cooling, which is as old as its creation. This process helped to cool more vapor into more water and helped to create our atmosphere, but we weren't called *Earth* yet.

Our Earth was then reshaped through volcanoes, earthquakes, weathering, etc. Billions of gallons of frozen water began melting, and geological forces shaped these. Suppose you venture to a part of Colorado and Utah, USA; you can see this geological history in person. You can visit Zion, Canyonlands, and Bryce Canyon National Parks and see extraordinary evidence about this cycle and its constant changes.

Years ago, my wife and I visited those national parks. We took pictures daily and saw a deterioration in the surface of the different rock layers. You can travel there and see what it's like today. You will see the evidence that the Earth was formed millions of years ago and that water covered all or most of it.

You can see these layers and remains of the fossils when life started to impact the earth and visualize what must have happened between those years and now. Changes in the earth are still happening, but it just occurs at a rate that is too slow for most of humanity to appreciate but know that it is still happening.

Time moves very slowly when we talk about the earth changing. Dinosaurs roamed our planet for at least 165,000,000 to 200,000,000 years. Land bridges, in some form or another, connected all of the lands on this planet. The Pamir Knot had a role to play in the separation of land masses. First, this knot was close to the Hindu Kush and the Himalayas mountain ranges. These are still among the highest mountains on earth.

Global plate tectonics is a generally accepted scientific theory that considers the Earth's lithosphere comprised of several tectonic plates interlocking with parts of the Earth's crust that float on our viscous upper mantle. These plates move toward each other through pressure, and then sometimes, they retreat away from each other due to the intense heat emanating from the core of the Earth.

Sixty-six million years ago, a cataclysmic event occurred! A giant meteor 7.5 miles wide collided with Earth, which wiped out 75% of all life on the planet. We can see this ring left in the rocks nearly everywhere around the earth, and approximately 3,000,000 years later, there was a rebirth of life.

Plantlife and trees appeared, the sun reappeared in the sky, and the Earth began to change. Other beings arrived along with Woolly Mammoths between 8,000,000 and 2,200,000 years ago after crossing a land bridge in Central America. Many of those animals were as long as six meters, stood over ten feet tall, and weighed more than two tons.

Some smaller animals could transport themselves by foot everywhere. At the same time, they searched for food, but there was soon to appear a significant separation of land masses which would not make movement easier for most creatures. This separation would make a difference.

Nearly all Ice Age creatures are now extinct because the climate has changed again. The ice melted, the Ice Age ended, and the Earth warmed. Giant Sloths made their way to this continent 2,200,000 ago after crossing a land bridge in Central America. They weighed almost four tons each! Today, in Southeast Asia, lemurs and other four-legged animals cling to trees. Still, the arrival of different beings and the appearance of planet-warming life led to the demise of the larger animals.

You can see preserved fossils of these early giant inhabitants of Southwestern America near what is now New Mexico near White Sands. The Giant Sloths were herbivores and stood as tall as some trees and were approximately five meters in length, larger than many bush elephants.

Smiledones, a large cat species, also flourished in middle North America. They had wide mouths and eight-inch fangs. They didn't last long and disappeared around ten thousand years ago. Giant sloths still existed but could not find enough food to survive.

The land around them was changing, and they sought different approaches to keep up with the changing environments.

With the changing environments, approximately 3,000,000 years later, animals went from walking on all fours to bipedalism. It became visible that hominids began walking upright instead of on all fours. That was significant, and less time had to be devoted to protection and travel. The idea of becoming sedentary interested them, and over some time, a long time by anyone's measurement, that idea took hold.

This rebirth took a long time. Early hominids, apes, and other foraging species appeared. Much evidence shows that our human race has descended from all of these people—starting in Africa and descending into sapiens and Neanderthals leaving Africa around 150,000 to 190,000 years ago.

Then, Australopithecines, Neanderthals, and others followed. This fact supports the claim of archeologists of which groups were inhabiting the European continent. The work of archaeologists gives us clues that these life forms have overlapped each other but in different areas.

Neanderthals were first discovered in Germany in the Neander Valley and had gained a bad reputation for being brutes huddled in cold caves while gnawing on bones and meat. However, further research and advances in archaeology, dating, genetics, and anthropology have revealed that the Neanderthals not only had bigger brains than us Sapiens but also walked upright and had a greater lung capacity. They were skilled toolmakers and big-game hunters who lived in large social groups, built shelters, traded jewelry, wore clothing, planted crops, and used heat to cook food. There also is evidence about them speaking complex languages. They even kept records and buried their dead.

What about here on the American continent? The archeological timeline of the Americas includes an 8000-year gap between the initial settlements and the subsequent development of those lands for farming. The settlers had been trying to convert the wilderness into farms that were terrible places to grow food. They attempted to make a life in nature for themselves and grow agricultural products from those newly cultivated lands.

The few people there saw newer arrivals come, and all of them were there to start a new life. Historians have hardly begun to study this time—they refer to it as archaic. However, the only thing ancient about it is that writers had referred to this as a time *when nothing happene*. They thought no change happened since none of it was witnessed, and hardly any of it had been reported by scholars.

North American archaeologists believe that the Clovis people were the first to reach the Americas about 11,500 years ago. The ancestors of the Clovis were thought to have crossed a land bridge linking Siberia to Alaska during the last ice age. They have also been named the Paleo-Indians.

Time passed, but it was passing by very slowly, and no one was there to mark that time's passing, but time just passed; one day melted into another. That would take more time, much more time. More of these groups, gatherers, and hunters, would continue, and they followed the food and life-supporting environments.

Approximately 12,000 years ago, the mammoth began to die off at the end of the last Ice Age. Six thousand years later, they became extinct. As humans evolved, animals started to shrink in size, and many of the large animals could not survive. The atmosphere became friendlier than it was for our earliest ancestors.

Hunters and gatherers emigrated to these areas and began setting up primitive homes, populating regions, and having children. This period encompassed more than 50% of those days when humans resided on this continent. This time was not uneventful, though.

Everything was happening, but it was happening slowly. There were no thoughts about long-term planning or even planning for tomorrow as they concentrated on each day. The concept of the formality of time was not relevant other than to that of seasons, moon phases, and the sunrise and sun-setting.

These days were not time-oriented, and each day was evolving as the change was slow and the passage of time was slow. But times were changing as humans acquired skills like farming, fishing, foraging, and other means of community survival. Clothing was being developed as these people began processing fibers from grasses and trees. Progress was slow. There were no clocks, no schedules, no calendars. The passage of time had no relevance at all!

With all of this going on, we found little to no communication between tribal groups. Our human ancestors killed many small animals after the warmer weather gave them fewer survival options. However, there was conflict on the earth about searching for food and establishing the protection needed to maintain life.

Were these early settlers looking for a change? People just did what they needed to do. No one offered advice, made suggestions, or told others what to do. There was no law, no government, no one offering advice or telling someone to stop what they were doing. No one outside your group/clan or tribe seemed to care who you were. No one considered your color, your thoughts, or your beliefs.

People were just trying to survive. They didn't impede anyone or try to change anyone's mind outside their group or clan. These people lived separately in indigenous tribes and didn't try to infringe or influence anyone. The concept of the community did not exist.

These were peaceful people. They were content. They started to develop pictorial language using signs. If there was any evidence of a spoken means of communication, that evidence has never been seen. They might have had common communication ways, but that has never been substantiated. They still had some means of connecting.

These were people, men, and women, living and maintaining their lifestyles. No one was there judging them or objecting to anything because there was no one to report what was happening. Things happened, but they only happened to those involved at the moment.

When hunting was poor, or fishing yielded no food, they did not stay around to complain. That would do them no good. They just moved away to some other place and continued to do what they were doing until they found other places to hunt, where they could find trees for shelter, and continued with their nomadic existence.

Thousands of years later, people built homes from the earthen soil around them. The sites of these mounds still exist today. They have been found in family units, and family to an anthropologist means economy, living together, reproduction, and burial.

Every society has a pattern of generational relationships, which we find each time we dig into the earth and reveal another clue to the human family. During one life, one occupies a series of states or roles associated with birth, maturation, and death.

We follow a biologically defined cycle. Humans are a rogue species as the anthropology of man; Change is possible. There is disappointment with the human race. The facts are forever true. We see groups come and go; societies vanish through war, disease, or possibly a combination. Still, ultimately human beings will continue this pattern as we see today, proving that we are not all that different from each other.

People continued to move North into these newly discovered lands. This new travel and occupation bring up a few questions.

When did conquering and warring with other groups begin? There is evidence that these changes occurred about 10,000 years ago. Based on the additional progress men and women made in establishing lives for themselves, they would go out and defend their community.

When this occurred, people looked for leadership and began to organize themselves in a managerial hierarchy. Progress may have proceeded in baby steps, but as their quality of life improved, more choices were found for more and more groups of people. Then people began to organize themselves into governments, hierarchies, monarchies, etc. For good or ill, people began to govern themselves to advance their thoughts about their future.

No one knew it then, but life would soon become more complicated; more people would come, and interactions would increase between these residents and the recent arrivals. Communication would begin in some form, and fundamental relations would begin. This evidence is supported until the last ice age, around 9700 BC.

The evidence of tribal warfare on the American continent wasn't reported until 9700 BC. Based on the archeological evidence, it appears that before this, there was no hint of bias, no hint of prejudice. This is interesting because ancient civilizations seem to have this in common with what was experienced on our continent.

The Norte Chico civilization in Peru is the oldest civilization in the Americas and one of the first six independent civilizations in the world. Moving forward in time from there, we find the Olmec, Aztec, Maya, and Inca peoples.

Here on this continent, the Olmec, named after the Olmec peninsula, was a group of people that began to form a society. They were from the Yucatan. The Olmecs (2500 to 400 BC) were a precursive force that identified many aspects that became a part of Mesoamerican civilization. Their culture was derived from several tribal cultures in the Yucatan portion of Mexico.

The Olmec were known for their intricate weaving of other cultures and identities as they combined aspects of different cultures with theirs; they were a heterogeneous culture that blended the addition of other peoples, languages, values, and customs into their own. They shared and borrowed with their neighbors. They were known for their massive stone heads carved from volcanic rocks such as basalt. They resided near Veracruz and Tabasco in Mexico, and around 400 BCE, the Olmecs created a diaspora that led to their evacuation of the Yucatan from Mexico. They moved north to lands that would eventually become part of America.

The Olmec people did not initially have that name. They were called the Olmec because of their relationship with the Aztec Nation. Olmec meant *rubber people*. They were hard-working, adventurous, and prosperous. They migrated north into lands that would one day become a part of America.

The Olmec people had to cope each day. They raised their children, found places to hunt, and they fell trees to provide wood for shelter. No one complained. Hundreds of years later, people moved in and built homes from the earth and the soil around them. Some of those homes still exist as mounds all across this continent.

Hundreds of years later, anthropologists and sociologists studied descendants of these early cultures and tried to make the point that they believed their role was to make the world safe for human differences.

Here is something of great significance. The history of the Olmec people established a life of democracy here on the American continent. According to Roger Atwood, evidence of Tlaxcala was a society that boasted of cities, order, and organization. Their egalitarian social structure was unsurpassed among known societies in ancient Mexico.

Unlike the Maya, the Tlaxcala had a comprehension of wealth and equality. They had a high standard of living based on their structure of common houses. So much was equal and orderly.

According to a recent article in Archaeology Magazine, some scholars believe Tlaxcallan's nonhereditary government system undermines the idea of democracy as a Western invention born in ancient Greece. This substantiates that Tlaxcala and other ancient societies in this hemisphere that had supported this system have been based on a democratic way of life.

When the Spanish arrived in this part of the world, they found that the people of Tlaxcallan had a collective, Republican-style government. Their distinctive urban landscape was first with this type of collaborative political organization.

This is more evidence that not only did people in the Ol* Worl* have the concept of equality to the best of their human abilities, but democracy was founded here, on the American continent, as well.

In school, we are taught that Columbus landed in the West Indies in 1492 and several more times. However, many thousands of people were already living in North America before he arrived. These people had roots. They had organized tribes, maybe even nations. They exhibited practical livelihoods like hunting, farming, and fishing. These people didn't call themselves In*ians. All Indian tribes referred to themselves as *the people*. Native Americans lived in America but didn't *iscover it either; they migrated there.

Most Native Americans had no idea that Columbus *iscovere* the land they had lived on for thousands of years when he claimed it for Spain. They just went on with their lives. His *iscovery* was irrelevant to them but essential to Isabella, the Queen of Spain. Columbus' discovery was only relevant to European imperialists.

Many early settlers who came to North America were looking for a change. Many came for different reasons, but they all had to focus on food, survival, and getting used to a new place where new people were residing.

There were choices that these early Americans could pursue, harness, and do work for themselves to improve the conditions under which they had to cope. It just took time, but these people had plenty of that. They still didn't have clocks, written calendars, or schedules. The passage of time was measured by sunrise and sunset, but it all had little relevance.

People were just people, and they could only really see as far as their society allowed them. Many people would stay within a few miles of where the community supported them.

If there is one connection of the human race, you stay connected for your survival. These small societies were not capable of forming formal laws and large organized governments because they were merely surviving with the group that they lived with.

Society didn't care who you were; no one cared about your thoughts or beliefs. People were just people going through the same things you were; surviving. No one cared to tell you what to do about your problems. They had their problems to deal with. No one was concerned with your beliefs.

People were just living their lives, raising their children, and loving their families. There were little to no arguments with other groups because as long as you stay within your community, all were relatively safe.

Everyone just continued with their lives. Tribes needed no courts, police, or formal governments. Everything was more straightforward then, everyone was trying to live their own lives in their way, and they did not demand anyone else change. By today's standards, that was remarkable.

As you read through this, what do you think? Is this a new perspective that causes you to pause and think? Remember that many people tell you what they want you to believe. But I urge you to look at the facts and evidence. Study things out and evaluate things.

When you listen to politicians, newscasters, journalists, and talk show hosts, they want you to think as they do.

Although there is no similarity between the lives of the Earth's later settlers and these people of earlier times, we can reflect on the commonality of what cultures had to experience. The baby steps that made adaptations and the speed with which the transformations occurred illustrate the expansion and growth of a people and its culture.

We must, however, make room for the truth. All of us are entitled to the right to have the same freedom as everyone else. This might be called *pervasive elegance*. Each of us is entitled to select our system of beliefs, and we should be allowed to make choices and attain them for ourselves. That is our right! The way other people perceive our differences is not the criteria. Native American civilizations were here before European settlers came to what would become America.

These English and European settlers expected more but were never prepared to offer parity and equality to others. There have been many instances where it became common for Native Americans to suffer because they did not look like, dress like, or think like Whites who settled in America.

Whites permitted these native Americans to enter their newly franchised schools when schools were established in later generations. Still, they were never made to feel welcome or considered equal.

In attempting to assimilate White offspring with children of Native Americans, the people who ran these schools even gave the native American children English names, cut their hair, and forbade them from speaking the languages their parents had taught them. They gave each a new name to drive them out of the culture they had been raised in and taught them a new language to speak and live with.

The impact on native American culture was immense. These children came out of this period of stress, hardly knowing who they were. America did not provide the means for healing and reconciliation for these Native Americans. America has done little to provide a path toward the truth from this story. The reality has not been dealt with, nor has anyone offered what the meaning of equality addresses in their lives. That is a tragedy, but we cannot change the past; we must learn from it.

This example raises the question, how will we ever find our path to the truth if we do not address equality and not teach equality? This is another example of perpetuating the idea of America to all of us without regard to differences so that we can create no confusion about teaching the truth to all of our young.

Hasn't this unfair treatment gone on long enough? People, even those who didn't look like each other, were still equal to those around them, experiencing the same things, and had hoped they would have similar outcomes as others experienced. The fabric of American history has been riddled with discrepancies. It is time to try to bring that habit to an end.

Isn't it time to realize that we are all in this thing called life together and that if all of us are going to make it to where we want to be, we have to make choices, be flexible and accept every one of us in the same way that we want to be accepted? Remember that even the Earth has been through change. Granted, it takes time to change, but there is evidence even down to the bedrock that change on Earth can and has happened and will continue.

Remember, we are all in this thing called *LIFE* together. Remember that no one is better than anyone else and that no one is less good than anyone! These are words to live by.

4

What Led Up to The Declaration of Independence

"Efforts and courage are not
enough without purpose."
– John Fitzgerald Kennedy.

Things happen, and things will work out. Many people who came before us believed that whatever is, is right! They shared the opinion that we should be satisfied with what we have and pursue our own lives, and we shouldn't fear for the future; in fact, we should not even be afraid of what might lie ahead.

To live with this concept of fear will lead to doom. We can be rational human beings because we want our society to be better than it is now.

We need *Secon▪ Chances.*

It's an extraordinary history that we have endured because of this hope. After all, an excellent education has been made possible by those provided with the opportunity to make their lives better and improve the possibility that our lives would be better.

Magna Carta

Magna Carta, otherwise known as *The Great Charter,* was issued by King John of England (r.1199-1216) and is one of the most famous documents in the world. In 1215, his nobles revolted against him, which was the practical solution to the political crisis he faced. The Magna Carta established that everybody, including the king, was *subject to the law* for the first time.

The Magna Carta remains a cornerstone of the British constitution, even with a third of the text deleted or rewritten. Sixty-three clauses have been written into the Magna Carta, but let's pay close attention to clause thirty-nine.

This clause gave all *free men* the right to justice and a fair trial. For the first time in history, the commoner might receive some justice. This ideal and other principles are echoed in the United States Bill of Rights (1791) and many other constitutional documents worldwide. The Universal Declaration of Human Rights (1948) and the European Convention on Human Rights (1950) also support the 39th clause:

> *No free man shall be seized or imprisoned, or stripped of his rights or possessions, outlawed or exiled, or deprived of his standing in any other way, nor will we proceed with force against him or send others to do so, except by the lawful judgment of his equals or by the*

> *law of the land. To no one will we sell, to no one deny or delay right or justice.* — Magna Carta

The Magna Carta (1215) had been written, and so had the Petition of Rights (1625). One was enacted into law before Thomas Hobbes's birth (in 1588), and the other became law during his lifetime. Therefore, he probably never thought about them. He did little more than accept what the few men he encountered accepted or expected, and perhaps no conversations took place.

The Enlightenment

Let's continue with a little more history: The Enlightenment. The Enlightenment emerged from Europe in the 18th century and represented a departure from the legitimacy of a government from a religious authority such as a theocracy or the divine right of kings.

What is the divine right of kings? It's been used by monarchs for centuries. They claim that their power was given to them by God, and if you questioned the monarch's authority, it was the same as questioning God's authority.

The history of *The Enlightenment* had a combination of impacts from the Scientific Revolution and the Protestant Reformation (a reform movement to remove corruption from the Roman Catholic Church). The Protestant Reformation created new Christian denominations.

The core Enlightenment values emphasized *liberty, individual rights, and reason.* The governments that reflected these values granted more freedom to the common people based on 'self-governance, natural rights, and natural law.'

A few understood the Enlightenment philosophy, including the 52 men who signed and influenced America's Declaration of Independence, the U.S. Constitution, and the Bill of Rights.

Three Enlightenment philosophers whose writings impacted the founding documents of the United States include English philosopher, scientist, and historian, Thomas Hobbes, French political philosopher Baron de Montesquieu, and English philosopher John Locke.

The Social Contract

Think about this. In England, between 1650 and 1670, life could only be described as terrible. During those years, rampant disease in primarily rural areas meant that residents had to endure fewer exchanges between neighbors.

In London, people believed the Petition of Rights (1625) was the chance to make a life for themselves and their families. The words of the Petition of Rights tried to assuage some of the annoying aspects of life under the Stuarts, and citizens had the perseverance to experience and find choices that would produce changes in their lives. Most were still burdened by dire poverty.

There were population increases away from the towns, and that did not help things. Most people were still illiterate. Trade under these circumstances was complex, but these conditions offered a chance to some in the mercantile system. Guilds were set up, which created some jobs, but not for all those who wanted them. Life was complex. The news was not available. Schools were hard to find, and education of any kind was limited.

Citizens offered their services to those who could afford to hire them. Birth rates increased, but the dire need for change would not diminish population growth or the expansion of towns. A slow-moving movement into urban areas was essential for people to find work to feed families.

London was expanding, and many people who fled agricultural poverty hoped to have more independent control over their lives and create a community. Soon even London disappointed them and left them without hope. New solutions were needed if they were going to be able to live a better life.

When chances presented themselves to these downtrodden folk, they left London's deplorable living conditions and found a second chance for themselves and their families by sailing west to the British colonies in America. They would have to work hard and start from scratch, but everything they earned, made for themselves, and built did not have to be shared with the ruling, land-owning aristocracy. It was theirs to keep, in theory.

It took time, but it was theirs. Those who came here to America did not know what to expect, so they would have to work hard and start from scratch. However, they had to do *something*. The life they were leaving behind held no unfulfilled promises, so they had to direct their future opportunities to the lands across the Atlantic. Determination grows as chances dwindled.

They left England because of the restraints they encountered as they longed to be free. Together, they felt they did not want to be limited in what they were able to achieve. They refused to accept the idea of control. That's what they had left behind in Europe; they didn't want that idea to be used again. They looked for freedom and wanted to enjoy that freedom without constraint.

In 1651, Thomas Hobbes (1588-1679) published his *Leviathan*. It wasn't forward-looking; he was trading hope for safety. He believed that man should be willing to *trade liberty for security*. Thomas Hobbes's way of thinking provided one of the first roadmaps to achieve what Jean-Jacques Rousseau and John Locke each created as a part of the concept of the *Social Contract.*

Hobbes suggested that the government should only provide a means to achieve safety and security. He added that the purpose of the government was to provide that safety based on the collective interest of its citizens.

It did not occur to Thomas Hobbes that all humanity should be considered: female, those of different sexual orientation, or anyone else regardless of the color of one's skin! As he referred to *citizens,* he thought they were only counted according to the law—White, male property owners. However, Hobbes did not mention all of these people were still members of society.

Hobbes failed to discuss a path ahead to achieve goals. It remained a task to be accomplished. He never delivered a sound, rational manner in his writings. He wrote about his thoughts but never dealt with any pragmatic sense about trying to achieve them.

Hobbes did say, however, that he "considered the origin of the state to be found in a contract through which every man might expediently give up himself for the benefit of all." He says that the law of nature is not law at all; it is "the qualities that dispose men to peace and obedience in the community."

With Hobbes, humanity's only right was to *preserve itself against ·estruction.* At the same time, John Locke was consumed with the idea that *all men live· in a con·ition of free·om an· equality un·er natural law.* John Locke stated, "Each possessed certain rights, such as the ownership of private property, and they should attempt to maintain their liberty."

Hobbes believed that the purpose of the *Social Contract* was to establish organized *Law an· Or·er* so that the "uncertainties of the state of nature could be replaced by the predictability of known laws and institutions, thus maintaining trust between all men."

In his *Secon♦ Treatise on Government,* Locke agreed with Hobbes about the *Rights of Man.* Political power was the source of authority necessary to make and enforce laws upon the political community.

However, unlike Hobbes, Locke believed that though men were *born free an♦ remaine♦ free,* "they were restrained by the law of nature" and that men were not inherently evil as Hobbes had suggested. Locke believed that man had, in fact, a natural morality, *Lex Naturalis,* which marks the state of nature with specific unwritten rules which obliges everyone to observe. Locke states, "The use of reason can teach all of humanity who will consult it that no man should try to bring harm to another."

With Thomas Hobbes, man's only right was to "preserve himself against others." Locke, however, was consumed with the idea that "all men lived in a condition of freedom and equality under natural law" and that each possessed *certain rights,* such as the "ownership of private property and their liberty."

The *Social Contract* then established and organized *Law an♦ Or♦er* so that the uncertainties of the state of nature would be replaced by the predictability of known laws and institutions, thereby creating and maintaining trust between all men.

French Political philosopher Baron de Montesquieu wanted to combine rationalism which emphasizes the universal with the historical method, and that "each unique individual is unlike all other men and that none of these men are abstract things."

Montesquieu is best known for advocating the separation of powers and checks and balances for an effective government (reflected in the U.S. Constitution). Montesquieu argued that "government should be set up so that no man need be afraid of another." He felt the people would be protected from an unjust government by separating political powers.

Montesquieu suggested separating political power among a legislature, an executive, and a judiciary; does that sound familiar? He defended a democratic form of government compared to a single monarch or similar ruler. He based this "model of the Constitution on the Roman Republic and the British constitutional system."

Montesquieu added that the Roman Republic had powers separated so that no one could *usurp* absolute power. However, John Locke's views are reflected in the U.S. Declaration of Independence, mainly focusing on nature and social compact law.

The few people who became aware of these events were never asked about their opinions; they just followed the choices others favored. That was, however, a step in the right direction. The thinking was only short-term. It remains that way—now, even more than ever.

Some people who became aware of these events were never offered a place at the table to share their opinions. It took the English over 400 years to get to this point, and England still wasn't finished. The Bill of Rights became part of the law of the land in 1689 when it replaced and improved upon the thoughts within the Magna Carta.

John Locke and Thomas Hobbes offered their opinions but were not alone. Jean-Jacques Rousseau provided, through *The Social Contract*, the idea that man can claim that by his view of natural liberty, each can have unlimited rights to everything that he can get his hands on. Still, he also gains civil liberty and property rights to all he possesses. Rousseau adds that *all men* are entitled to that.

Rousseau disagreed with Montesquieu's conclusion. In 1762, he wrote the *Social Contract*, the central issue of which is a political obligation.

> "The problem is to find and form an association with others which will defend and protect each of us with the whole force of the person and goods belonging to each associate, and in which each, while uniting himself with all, may still obey himself alone and remain as free as before." –Jean-Jacques Rousseau.

At the beginning of his epic work, Rousseau's man is born free. "Everywhere man is in Chains." How do we begin to deal with that dichotomy?

Rousseau is not as gloomy as Hobbes, but he is not as optimistic as Locke. He advocates the *Social Contract* because it provides security with a collective association. Still, it also combines protection with liberty with the end an individual had before entering into the contract.

Rousseau continues that "man in nature is guided by instinct only, whereas, in society, morality and justice are goals side by side." This early philosophy was converted to modern practical use in the hands of John Locke (1632-1704), who was used as a contrast to Thomas Hobbes.

Their contrasting views consisted of doctrines that help explain the significance of ideas and the thoughts about the diversity of politics that promote change.

Although Hobbes was a defender of absolutism and Machiavellianism, Hobbes believed his views should share in this spotlight of philosophy. When Hobbes published his answer to reverse the pervasive instability throughout the continent, his answers profoundly shocked many of his contemporaries.

Hobbes started with a pessimistic proposition that men are selfish, antagonistic, and downright hostile to each other! Because of these flaws, Hobbes denied the laws of morality. He thought that man was immoral because most men had an innate lust for power.

Without law, there would be no universally recognized standard of Justice. Hobbes described man's life without a government as "helpful, poor, nasty, brutish and short." His conclusions were comparable and similar to those of religious theologians of those early days.

Hobbes believed that these evil propensities of the excesses of men necessitated the existence of a strong, energetic, powerful government. Hobbes gave contract theory a purely secular interpretation accepted for many years. Today, however, that interpretation is under renewed scrutiny.

Later, John Stuart Mill, in his *On Liberty*, added that it fell to civil liberty and its protection that would balance the scales of Justice. This concept would protect each citizen against arbitrary acts by the government against minorities via "obtaining recognition of specific communicated ideas called political liberties or rights."

The Declaration of Independence

Let's transfer these concepts to the Declaration of Independence and see if they stand up today. On January 9th, 1776, Thomas Paine stated, "at one time, it was believed that it was only *common sense* that an island could not rule a country."

Thomas Jefferson added that the principles of our revolutionary enterprise emphasized the *self-evident* nature of the principles at stake with his opening gambit found in the first words of our Declaration of Independence; "We hold these truths to be self-evident."

However, to this day, there is still something missing. When Jefferson wrote the opening words *We, the People*, to whom was he referring? He wrote those words by himself. Why wasn't that person ever identified if he had written those words with someone else? Then too, why were these three words included? Was Jefferson using an editorial *we*?

Blacks, Native Americans, or any other race, would fall into a subcategory and were not considered. Did Jefferson believe these words applied to Blacks, women, and native Americans? Or was it assumed that once a woman married, there was no need for her to individually have rights because she would be part of the union with that man?

This is what I'm trying to wake you up to. In fact, how long has telling the truth about this part of our past been customary for all of America? The Declaration of Independence stands as a hypocritical statement because it pertained, at the time, to only White males. Wars have indeed been fought, and amendments have been made to allow those words to cover more people—and that is at least something, but it should have been *ma e from the start.*

Now that you have the background of all the philosophies, I would like to ask you about the literacy of America at this time. If we take Thomas Jefferson's word, "Educate and inform the whole mass of the people... They are the only sure reliance for the preservation of our liberty." That sounds like he was addressing all people. But again, no, that was not true. He was only referring to White males. They were allowed to be educated at the time.

Let's look at this little bit of history. How many American settlers were literate? That number was less than 30% of the entire country. That means that most Americans at the time of the American Revolution could not read or could write. Many religious groups encouraged the Quaker's literacy so that they could read the bible but only encouraged boys and men to read. Girls and women were rarely taught.

Back in the 17th and 18th centuries, why would you need a library if you couldn't read or write? How many of our forebears were able to write? If you can read and write, you need paper, a pen, perhaps even notebooks, etc. If you do not know these things, how do you learn?

Yet elite men like Jefferson, Franklin, Madison, etc., had books and were well-read, self-taught, and formally educated. But what about everyone else? Jefferson even collected books and had the time to maintain those books that he brought home from Europe every time he returned to America.

In 1776, after the Declaration of Independence was sent to the printer for publication, Benjamin Rush overheard a conversation between two members of the Second Continental Congress. One of the two gentlemen was Elbridge Gerry of Massachusetts. The other person in that conversation was Benjamin Harrison of Virginia.

Harrison was overheard by a passerby when he said, "when we are all hung for what we are doing, what will all of this matter?" The impact of those 55 men has impacted the millions who have lived after them.

Later, Washington added that "the citizens of America would now be possessed of absolute freedom and independence." Mr. Washington omitted another opinion when he did not pursue the most critical questions of *why* and *how!* What was missing was the more important answer to the question.

Washington, at this time, never considered that all colonists would not be treated equally or that some might never have the same rights as everyone else. But then, Washington never brought up the subject of the Black minority already established in the colonies. Washington never thought that Blacks were equal to Whites. Of course, no one considered women or Native Americans equal to White men. Therefore, from the outset, we were never supposed to have the same rights as everyone else if we did not believe in equality.

They further added that "when any government becomes destructive of these ends, it is the right of the people to alter or abolish it and institute a new government with a foundation on such principles as they deem practical to affect their safety and [provide for everyone's] happiness." They had a closing which said, "the government should not be changed for light and transient causes."

So, now it is more than 246 years after we were promised equal representation and an equal right to participate in the process offering all of us a role in overseeing this country's success. Isn't it possible that enough time has gone by and we have learned enough things about all of us who live in the country that we should atone for the mistakes that we made over 200 years ago and try to right the wrongs that we created?

If a government tries to accomplish anything and creates abuses and usurpations in that attempt, then "the people have a right and a duty to throw off such a government." Perhaps we should consider our recent history and invigorate or intensify our participation energies.

Voting is one way. John Adams was not up to the task as a European history student with a law degree. He believed our problems were overwhelming, but he took another road and attempted to limit participation in our voting.

By trying to restrict access to the government and restricting free speech, he was not tuned to what the majority sought. Therefore, the people denied him a second term. Jefferson stayed clear of these issues. He added platitudes to the conversation, but that was all he could do because he owned hundreds of enslaved Black Americans in our country.

After winning the battles of the American Revolution, the Treaty of Paris was signed; our Independence was established, and we were well on our way. Then there was England. Secretly, the propertied gentry attempted to convene a meeting and reconcile questions about the government and its relationship with our former mother country, but that didn't go very far.

Two million White male colonists populated the lands of the newly independent colonies. Some of these were tenants, but most were not. Just think about the people living here in America then, and if those words of the Declaration of Independence really would have applied to all—think of how much further we would be to-day. But alas, children, teenage boys, women, Blacks, and Native Americans were taken into account for this freedom.

The governors of these thirteen colonies decided to convene a secret meeting in Philadelphia to discuss how to improve the workings of the government under the Articles of Confederation.

Invitations were sent out to those on that list of invitees. What hubris! At best, this meeting was hardly a democratic event. The list of invitations included so few people. Almost no one showed up for this meeting.

Little has been changed, and even though there are more citizens in our country, when will the doors be opened so that a majority of us are permitted to participate in our democracy? We need a peaceful movement of citizens to lead the way! But before we start the whole movement towards our *Secon* *Chances,* we need to give a little more history and foundation.

Chapter 5 will expand your mind as you read through the exchange at the Constitutional Convention.

5

The Constitutional Convention

"When I dare to be powerful,
to use my strength in the
service of my vision, then it
becomes less and less important whether I am afraid."
–Audre Lorde.

Chapters 5-7 are the crucial portion of why America is what it is today. I have gathered information from original documents from the convention in which delegates said what they did and why. I will present some actual scripts and verbal exchanges at the Constitutional Convention.

This establishes that the fifty-two men who started the country were the only ones involved. Very few knew what was going on and that these were the only men who set up the Constitution as it stands today, complete with its flaws, and bear the full responsibility for our beginnings.

The rule provided "that no copy be taken of any entry on the journal during the sitting of the house, without leave of the house." Those members only were to be permitted to inspect the journal. Nothing spoken was to be printed or otherwise published or communicated without the permission of the entire convention.

James Madison has been given most of the credit for the thorough note-taking at the Constitutional Convention. However, Rufus King, James McHenry, William Pierce, William Paterson, and Alexander Hamilton also took notes of varying degrees of detail and length. What I have here is based on those notes.

The debate began, and two groups were formed. Delegates from Virginia presented a plan for the convention called the *Virginia Plan*. Paterson of New Jersey presented the *New Jersey Plan*.

1. Large State groups favored a genuine national government but opposed equal representation of the states in Congress. These states were Massachusetts, Pennsylvania, Virginia, North and South Carolina, and Georgia.
2. The small state group advocates the principles of equal representation.

Someone or group added to consider these resolutions and address the discussion. The Articles of Confederation had proposed equal representation in Congress. Connecticut, New Jersey, Maryland, Delaware, and New York were on board.

On May 30th, the convention adopted a resolution to create a national government. This government consists of a supreme legislative branch, a judiciary, and an executive.

A majority vote of the states carried this motion, and the convention never turned its back on the resolve which colonial experience had taught the delegates. That resolve was necessary to preserve liberty, and the ensuing debate and arguments centered on how this would be done, but it remained the express purpose of the convention.

The first significant discussion was between Virginia and New Jersey plans. Connecticut joined the large state group to vote down the New Jersey Plan. Maryland remained divided. This first issue would become the battleground.

Bitter debates followed between delegates Read of Delaware and Gouverneur Morris of Pennsylvania over the motion that equal representation in Congress, which prevailed under the Articles of Confederation, should continue within the new structure being considered.

Read responded that "delegates were restrained from offering their consent because it would not maintain the quality of congressional representation. If such a change should be voted in, it might become the duty of the Delaware delegates to withdraw from the convention."

Morris stated that "the valuable assistance of these men could not be lost without real concern. Still, the change proposal was a fundamental article in the national government debate that could not be dispensed with!"

The convention devoted its attention to considering these proposals and the manner of election of the various government officers.

In the case of the presidency, the conventional delegates spent much more time considering the structure and frequency of presidential elections and the length of tenure of the president's office and less time outlining the actual powers vested in the presidency.

The case of the Judiciary was brought up, and they were much more concerned with the manner of selecting the members of the Judiciary under the Constitution. Along with William Penn, they believed that "governments, like clocks, go from the motion men give them so that by them they are ruined too. Wherefore governments rather depend on men than men should depend on governments. Let men be good, and the government cannot be bad; if it is ill, they will cure it. But if men are bad, let the government be never so good; they will try to warp and spoil to their turn." This is significant because it introduced the idea that corrupt leaders would absolutely corrupt the government, so the appointments or choices of the Justices of the courts needed to be made carefully and intentionally with forethought and care.

Continuing the conversation about congressional delegates, Madison protested. He said, "It is not just to allow Virginia, sixteen times the size of Delaware, an equal vote as all other colonies were allowed."

Delaware's delegates retaliated with the idea that it would not be safe for Delaware's citizens if Virginia were allowed sixteen times as many votes as were appropriated. Paterson of New Jersey said, "he would not feel safe with five votes when Virginia had sixteen."

Ellsworth of Connecticut suggested the establishment of a Congress of two houses. One with equal representation and the other with representation based upon population. Benjamin Franklin endorsed Ellsworth's point of view.

A compromise committee deliberated over the possibilities and reported in favor of a bicameral national legislature. The House of Representatives was chosen based on population, and the Senate, where representation was equal for each state, would have two senators.

Bedford of Delaware rose and said to his feet, "Pretenses to support ambition are never wanting, gentlemen. I do not trust you. If you possess the power, abuse cannot be checked, and what would prevent you from exercising your power could lead to our destruction, which might happen sooner than you think. Powers, who would take us by the hand."

Rufus King of Massachusetts replied, "I am concerned for what fell from the mouth of the gentleman from Delaware. Take a foreign power by the hand? I am sorry that he mentioned it, and I hope he can excuse it from himself on the score of passion."

Let's regroup. What were Rufus King, Read of Delaware, and Gouverneur Morris of Pennsylvania debating over?

Remember that the first U.S. national government began under the Articles of Confederation, which was adopted in 1781. This document said nothing about slavery. It left the power to regulate slavery, as well as most powers, to the individual states.

Now with the Constitutional Convention, the subject must be faced. The outline for the new government would have three branches — executive, judiciary, and a two-house legislature. This was agreed to, but the challenge between the Carolinas and the north was how to represent the people with the two-house legislature.

States with large populations wanted representation in both houses of the legislature to be based on population. However, according to the ruling, you were already disadvantaged if your state had a small population. You can see by all of the quotes above how long this debate carried on—eleven days.

When it came to a vote, the compromise was carried by a majority of only one. There were six votes for the motion, and there were five votes against it. Since the rule provided that a majority vote could prevail in adopting any provisions to the Constitution, this vote of six to five resulted in the first *Great Compromise*.

In the end, the delegates agreed to the *Great Compromise*. The legislative branch, called the House of Representatives, would be based on population. The other, the Senate, would have two members from each state. Now both large and small states would be fairly represented—or would it?

The *Great Compromise* included a colossal problem that split the convention into North-South lines. The issue was: Should *enslave people* count as part of the population? How dare the 55 men in the room even suggest it! They wanted to have their cake and eat it too, as the saying goes.

The *cake* (so to speak) that the delegates eventually compromised and stated was that "each enslaved person would count as *three-fifths* of a person." Enslaved people were considered property, yet for this *Great Compromise* to work, they suddenly needed enslaved people to count—or at least a portion of the population. It just sickens me to think about it—shame on them.

Immediately following this *Great Compromise*, another controversy erupted: *What should be done about the slave trade and importing new slaves into the United States?* Ten states had already outlawed it. Many delegates heatedly denounced it (yet still practiced it). And three states threatened to leave if slavery was abolished.

The small states, most of which resided in the north, had one driving force: to form this new government. They eventually formed a special committee. And there, worked out another compromise: *Congress would have the power to ban the slave trade, but not until 1800.* The convention voted to extend the date to *1808.* They *kicke♦ that can ♦own the roa♦,* as the saying goes.

Finally, a significant issue involving slavery confronted the delegates. Southern states wanted other states to *return escape♦ slaves.* To give a short history, the Articles of Confederation had not guaranteed this. However, when Congress adopted the Northwest Ordinance (we will get into this in the chapter about Washington), there was a clause promising that slaves who escaped to the Northwest Territories would be returned to their owners.

This was the evidence needed in this debate, and the delegates placed a similar fugitive slave clause in the Constitution. This was a deal with New England states. So in exchange for the fugitive slave clause, the New England states got concessions on shipping and trade. How did this happen? These were people, not property! However, the push for *goo♦s an♦ property* ruled again.

These three compromises on slavery had severe effects on the nation. The small states hoped that slavery would die out, but only five years after these debates, the Cotton Gin was invented, and money now poured in from this evil institution. Enslaved people had just been strapped with another chain around their ankles. The only course of action to correct all of these compromises would have to be war.

Our Constitution, it is said, still stands as *a Beacon on the Hill.* Today it is still considered that way, but why is that the case?

The following pages will point toward reconsidering what we have done and discuss what we might do. What if we had a second constitutional convention in the coming years? We need to involve most of America to participate and not restrict participation to less than the sixty White men who discussed, debated, and wrote up our Constitution but did not remove the pitfalls that were possible for future generations.

We must provide a path for all Americans to participate and not exclude those who don't own property, and we should not exclude people who are not wealthy. White men should not be the only people who are allowed to participate.

The high ideals, platitudes, and language referred only to White men! No other choices were considered! We have to be better than that! If we want all Americans to remain Americans, we must be more inclusive with open doors for all of us who wish to participate. And some of those can be foreign-born human beings who decided to emigrate to America independently.

Some people and groups are trying to stall our efforts. Others have said that we have already reached the summit of political reasoning and eloquence. They started our government and would now no longer be powerless. According to the paperwork, all would benefit from the 1787 attempt, but the results of that convention have not been able to provide a path for the equal existence of all Americans!

Some have said that we now live in an America where millions are dying needlessly, and we, as a nation, are still feeble in the fact that we do not, even today, possess the will to fulfill those promises of our preamble.

Between 1783 and 1787, there was no apparatus to prepare the new government with a sound way to raise money to establish a basis for that government. Without money, those who set up our government provided no financial system.

There was no plan to allow this new startup government room, provide a cushion, or initiate any financial transactions. The government then had no security, nothing that they could fall back on or use to create the government's business. They didn't want to establish talks about fair taxation for everyone so that they could establish a new government on a sound financial basis or even consider providing funds to expand the reach of the new government.

In the 18th century, people just didn't think about the future. They knew nothing about what was going on in the world. Our Founding Fathers never explained their thoughts so that people could follow them in future generations. They only spoke of ideas but provided no pathways to attain those ideals.

They did not talk about education in public. They spoke only about themselves and thought only about themselves—remember, all of them were men. They did not consider the women in this country; they didn't even regard their wives as equal to themselves. They did not conceive of making any efforts that it would take to make sense for their children and other generations to follow. They simply remained as ideals and goals.

America was an idea founded on the principles of the Enlightenment, stemming from the Age of Reason. They believe in the ideas and ideals of this Enlightenment. In the early days of our country in the 18th century, election days were not limited to one day. Many of those allowed colonies and later states to enable their citizens to vote, but they had weeks to fill in their ballots. We should emulate that concept and try to keep all eligible voters in mind and give them a chance to participate. Perhaps we should lengthen the voting period in this country. How else will we ever attain the government of the people?

In the 17th century, almost everyone owned a gun. It was for hunting and protection. I think they also used their guns to expand slavery. They thought about what new land they could take. They thought about only what was pertinent to them. They gave no thought to the Constitution. They thought about how the Constitution protected their rights to own guns, but they didn't believe that guns would ever be a problem in the society that they were creating.

Now ask yourself, based on everything that you have read, how close are we to achieving the goals of the Preamble of our Constitution—that everyone can achieve equality? Have we achieved tranquility? Have we reached the blessings of liberty for ourselves and our posterity?

James Madison wrote about ideals, but he did not allow those ideas to be provided for everyone. His ideas about the basic tenets of our democracy were incompatible with his definition of liberty and were never made available to everyone. Even the free exercise of religion for everyone was not mentioned.

We should reconsider the life tenure of our judges and limit them to a specific number of years as a term for them to serve. Perhaps twenty years should be a starting point to allow new thoughts and different rationales to become part of our living jurisprudence.

The basis of this authority must always reside with the people. Why shouldn't we reconsider Rousseau's thoughts that everything should be decided by the people and *not* by appointments made by political parties? Why should we include other people who don't represent *the people* but only consider what *they, themselves,* think?

We are not all 'of the people' but just us. But the people get to write the guide as to what standards we should set for the future. Those voters get into the position to indicate how we should proceed in a democracy.

Let's look into what democracy is. Ask yourself this question, "Why should *the people* rule? Is democracy better than aristocracy or monarchy? Perhaps, as Plato argues in the *Republic,* the best government would be led by a minority of the most highly qualified persons—an aristocracy of "philosopher-kings.," if you will.

What reasons could be given to show that Plato's view is wrong? Isn't that how America was set up—meaning a select few created the documents and policies that we all live under? Yes, amendments have involved more people, but shouldn't it have started that way in the first place?

The people get to write the guide about standards for the future. Those voters move to get us into the position so we can find the path to proceed in our democracy. They can determine authority and move us in the direction where we can take a primary role in managing our democracy. This should permanently reside in the people themselves. People in this country should not restrict access to the ballot, or we will never maintain a democracy.

Honesty, integrity, and other values are worthwhile human goals. However, our Founders only thought about themselves and their male children. We are now paying the price for their patriarchal views. Even today, as we try to change how we do things, we still have to hear the opinions of those who do not want us to change. That is why many of us have a downhill view of the future of America.

Another thought to add to the mix is that the writers of our Constitution started by stating goals for the Constitution that they were offering the American people to live by. Those original goals were to *form a perfect union,* but if we didn't even have a genuine *Union,* we would never have a perfect one.

Those few attendees who signed the document we lived by and offered it to the states to endorse weren't perfect. No one is perfect, so how could we have a perfect union? Ergo how could we ever improve it so we could approach the ideal of perfection?

Let's get real! The Preamble had five goals: "to form a more perfect Union, establish justice, ensure domestic tranquility, provide for the common defense, promote the general welfare, and secure the blessings of liberty to ourselves and our posterity".

Many of us can cover 80% of those goals, but they have never been achieved by every man, woman, and child! We are not even close to having our entire society enjoy this because we have not done the work. Remember, we are so divided; how can we ever get a majority to push forward that effort?

But, we must provide a path for knowledge and understanding. We must seek to take *Secon Chances* and try to make the second time better so that we can start to heal because right now, people are hurting.

> William Penn once offered these words, "Time is what we want most, but time is what we use worst!" Those words were written over two hundred years ago! Time is infinite. We make time for this and plan to use time better, but we don't. We can still get this going. Let's get started.

England experienced the same growing pains as America. To me, however, the problem could have been addressed in 1787. So, too few attendees at the convention were educated enough to judge what they were saying without any context. They never considered options. In their discussions, they never considered the repercussions their petty arguments produce and would those arguments withstand the test of time.

Our framers endorsed the idea of domestic tranquility but did *not* advance it so that it is available for all citizens to live in peace.

They could never have predicted tranquility because they never thought about the significance of what they were doing and what that word meant. They didn't establish enough ways to make it happen. They never even thought to ask about those Americans who were not them and what they would have thought about what they were doing.

Wouldn't it be nice if we could get people's approval about the job we had accomplished? And wouldn't we be happy if people agreed with us? Even if they weren't pleased, perhaps they had another choice to offer, but nobody gave them a chance.

Equality is less evident to all of us if we all have it because all men cannot live with just the ideals that exist in our Constitution. That was because what was accomplished in 1787 wasn't great. That's why we must suggest courses for future citizens of this country.

We may have all been created equally, but that ideal has disappeared. With those words about equality, we should strive as we have never done to become more inclusive so that we can all prevail together.

6

Script For The Constitutional Convention

"The road to success is not easy to navigate, but with hard work, drive and passion, it's possible to achieve the American dream."
–Tommy Hilfiger.

Dear Reader,

What you are about to read has never been printed in any available books. I have a copy of the original document—as it is typed here, it is as it was written.

Why do I put this in my book? I want to give you proof and evidence about the actual words from the Constitutional Convention in Carpenter's Hall and give them context. Once you have read this, please consider the importance of the words and who they excluded from this crucial Constitutional Convention.

Sincerely,

Jeffrey Ellner

Opening scenes of the Constitutional Convention...

1. The first order of this convention is the electing of a presiding officer.
2. At that first session on May 25th, 1787, Robert Morris of Pennsylvania placed into nomination the name of George Washington for president of the convention.
3. John Rutledge of South Carolina seconded the motion.
4. George Washington was unanimously elected.
5. Washington was then conducted to The Chair by both Morris, and Rutledge Madison says that Washington "stood to thank the convention for the honor that they had conferred on him; reminded them of the novelty of the scene of business in which he was to act, lamented his want of better qualifications and claimed the indulgence of the House for the involuntary errors which his inexperience might occasion."
6. Major William Jackson was named secretary. He was actually literate.
7. A committee was appointed to present the rules of the convention.
8. Each state was given one vote.
9. Seven states constituted a quorum.

10. Most states could prevail on any question that would bind the rest of the members.

11. The convention adopted the following rule: every member, rising to speak, shall address the president; while that member was speaking, no other participant shall pass between him and the body, or hold discourse with another, or read from a book, pamphlet, or paper, or any printed material or manuscript.

12. A rule was adopted to lock the doors of the convention hall and provide secrecy of its proceedings.

The following is a list of delegates who participated in the Constitutional Convention of 1787:

New Hampshire: John Langdon; Nicholas Gilman

Massachusetts: Rufus King; Nathaniel Gorham; Elbridge Gerry: Mr. Strong

Connecticut: William Samuel Johnson; Roger Sherman; Oliver Ellsworth

New York: Alexander Hamilton; Yates; W. Lansing

New Jersey: William Livingston; David Brearly; William Paterson; John Dayton

Pennsylvania: Benjamin Franklin; Thomas Mifflin; Robert Morris; George Clymer;

Thomas Fitzsimmons; Jarod Ingorsol; James Wilson; Gouverneur Morris.

Delaware: John Dickinson; Gunning Bedford; George Read; Richard Basset; Jacob Broom

Maryland: Luther Martin; James McHenry; Daniel of St. Thomas Jenifer; Daniel Carrol

Virginia: George Washington; George Mason; James Madison; John Blair; Edmund Randolph

North Carolina: William Blount; Richard Dobbs Spaight; Hugh Williamson; William Davey; John Martin

South Carolina: John Rutledge; Charles Cotesworth Pinckney; Charles Pinckney; Pierce Butler

Georgia: William Few; Abraham Baldwin; Williar Pierce; William Houston

By The Convention of Hampshire County (before the Constitutional Convention)

These grievances of a Massachusetts county are characteristic of the rural classes throughout New England at this period. The convention was one of the opening scenes of Shay's Rebellion.

At a meeting of delegates from fifty towns in the county of Hampshire, in a convention held at Hatfield, in said county, on Tuesday, the 22nd day of August (1786), continued by adjournments until the 25th, etc. voted that this meeting was constitutional. From a thorough conviction of great uneasiness, the convention subsisted among the people of this county and Commonwealth.

Then went into an inquiry for the cause. Upon mature consideration, deliberation, debate, many grievances, and unnecessary burdens now lying upon the people are the sources of that discontent so evidently discoverable throughout this Commonwealth. Among which the following articles were voted as such:

1. The existence of the Senate.
2. The current mode of representation.
3. All the civil officers of the government, not annually elected by or of the people, in the General Court assembled.
4. The existence of the Courts of Common, pleas, and general sessions of the peace
5. The present mode of appropriating the impost and excise taxes
6. Unreasonable grants were made to some of the officers of the government.
7. The current model of paying governmental securities.
8. The present model was adopted for the payment and speedy collection of the last tax.
9. The current model of taxation as it operates unequally between the polls and estates and between landed and mercantile interests.
10. The want of a sufficient medium of trade to remedy the mischiefs arising from the scarcity of money.
11. The General Court sat in the town of Boston.
12. The neglect of the settlement of essential matters depending between the Commonwealth and Congress, relating to monies and averages.
13. They voted that this convention recommends to the several towns in this country that they instruct their Representatives, to use their influence in the next General Court, to have emitted a bank of paper money, subject to depreciation, making it tender in all payments, equal to silver and gold, to be issued to call in the Commonwealth's securities.
14. Voted, That whereas several of the above articles of grievances arise from defects in the Constitution; therefore, a revision of the same ought to occur.

15. Voted that this convention recommends to the inhabitants of this county that they abstain from all mobs and unlawful assemblies until a constitutional method of redress can be obtained.
     *Note that no plans to deal with differences of opinion were mentioned!

This is the first failure of the Confederation (1787). John Jay's career gave him authority to speak upon the failings of the confederation. He had been president of Congress, minister to Spain, negotiator of peace with England, and during the last four years of the Confederation, he was secretary of foreign affairs.

The following are extracts from a letter written to George Washington.

By Secretary John Jay to George Washington *New York, January 7th, 1787* (4 months before the Constitutional Convention)

Mr. Presi•ent,

The situation of our affairs calls not only for reflection an• pru•ence but for exertion. What is to be •one? Is a common question not easy to answer? Woul• it give any further •egree of power to Congress to •o the business?

I am much incline• to think it woul• not, for, among other reasons, there will always be members who will fin• it convenient to make their seats subservient to partial an• personal purposes. Those who may be able an• willing to concert an• promote useful an• national measures will sel•om

be unembarrasse♦ by the ignorance, preju♦ices, fears, or intereste♦ views
of others.

In a large bo♦y, secrecy an♦ ♦ispatch will be too uncommon; foreign
an♦ local influence will frequently oppose an♦ sometimes prostrate the
worst (wisest?) measures. As the many ♦ivi♦e blame an♦ ♦ivi♦e cre♦it, too
little portion of either falls to each man there to affect him strongly, even
in cases where the whole blame of the cre♦it must be national. It is not
easy for those to think an♦ feel like sovereigns accustome♦ to thinking
an♦ feeling as subjects....

Shall we have a king? Not in my opinion, while other experiments
remain untrie♦. Might we not have a governor-general limite♦ in his
prerogatives an♦ ♦uration? Might not Congress be ♦ivi♦e♦ into an upper
an♦ lower house - the former appointe♦ for life, the latter annually an♦
let the governor-general (to preserve the balance) with the a♦vice of a
council, forme♦ for that only purpose, of the great ju♦icial officers, have a
negative on their acts? What powers shoul♦ be grante♦ to the government
so constitute♦ is a question that ♦eserves much thought.

I think the more, the better the states retaining only so much as may
be necessary for ♦omestic purposes an♦ all their principal officers, civil
an♦ military, being commissione♦ an♦ removable by the national govern-
ment....

Would it not be better for Congress plainly and in strong terms
to declare that the present Federal Government is inadequate to
the purposes for which it was instituted? They forbear to point out
its particular defects or ask for an extension of any particular
powers. But that in their opinion, it would be expedient for the
people of the states without delay to appoint state conventions
with the sole and express power of appointing deputies to a general

convention who should take into consideration the Articles of Confederation and make such alterations, amendments, and additions as to them should appear necessary and proper?

No modifications in the government should, I think, be made nor, if attempted, will easily take place unless deducible from the only source of just authority – the People.

Preparations for the Convention (1787)

Mason was a delegate from Virginia. He was prominent in the debates, advocated popular measures, denounced the slave trade, and finally refused to sign the Constitution because of its aristocratic tendencies. This letter was addressed to his son.

By Delegate George Mason, from Virginia

The expectations an• hopes of all the Union center on this Convention. Go• grant that we may be able to concert effectual means of preserving our country from the evils which threaten us. I hope there will be more remarkable unanimity an• less opposition, except for the little States that were first apprehen•e•. The most prevalent i•ea is a negative upon all such laws as they shall ju•ge contrary to the interest of the fe•eral Union.

A negative in the principal states seems to be a total alternation of the present fe•eral system an• substituting a great national council or parliament consisting of two branches of the legislature, foun•e• upon the legislatures a sufficient portion of the principles of proportionate representation, with full legislative powers upon all subjects of the Union; an• an executive; an• to make the several state legislatures subor•inate to the national, by giving the latter the power of a negative upon all such laws as they shall ju•ge contrary to the interest of the fe•eral Union.

It is easy to foresee that there woul• be much •ifficulty in organizing a government on this great scale an• at the same time reserving to the state legislatures a sufficient portion of power for promoting an• securing the prosperity an• happiness of their respective citizens.

Proportionate representation, with the full legislative government upon the powers on all of the Union an• an executive, an• to make the several States subor•inate to the national, by giving the letter the prerogative upon all such laws as they shall ju•ge contrary to the interests of the fe•eral Union.

It is easy to foresee that there will be much to •o in organizing a government on this great scale an• at the same time, reserving to the State legislatures a sufficient portion of power for promoting an• securing the prosperity an• happiness of their respective citizens.

Philadelphia to consider the merits of revising the Articles of Confederation or writing an entirely new Constitution. It was decided that the delegates should write a new Constitution.

In May of 1787, the members of the Constitutional Convention met in Philadelphia to consider the merits of revising the Articles of Confederation or writing an entirely new Constitution. It was decided that the delegates should write a new Constitution.

The Chairman of the convention then recognized the representative from Virginia.

By Edmund Randolph, from Virginia

Mr. Chairman, fellow •elegates. All of us present realize an• un•er-stan• the sacre• an• honore• purpose which has brought us together in this buil•ing. We are charge• with a •uty important not only to us but also to future generations. We are charge• with abolishing the evils un•er which our people have •welle• •ue to the Articles of Confe•eration. We are charge• with establishing a strong government that woul• give our people a stable foundation upon which they might grow, expand, and flourish.

The new government must be able to legislate in all cases in which the separate states are incompetent or in which the harmony of the U.S. may be interrupted by the exercise of individual legislation; to negative all laws passed by the several states, contravening in the opinion of the National Legislature, the articles of union, or any treat subsisting under the authority of the union, and to call forth the force of the union against any member of the union failing to fulfill its duties under the Articles thereof.

Therefore, I place a plan before this convention to provide for a strong government. The government comprises three parts: a Congress to make the laws, a branch to enforce those laws, and a system of Courts to ensure that the people receive justice under these laws. The Congress will be divided into two branches – an upper house and a lower house. The members of the Upper House are to be elected directly by the people, and each state is to have a set number of Representatives according to its population. The members of this house are then to elect the lower house members. Our plan would establish a central government based upon the people's votes; it would issue more power to the central government and weaken the state's power. Yet it would also strengthen our country as never before.

Several convention members felt that this union plan would prioritize the larger states over the smaller ones.

Therefore, several days later, William Paterson presented his method of the union.

By William Paterson, from New Jersey

Mr. Chairman, •istinguishe• •elegates: We, of the small states, have given much consi•eration to Mr. Ran•olph's plan of union, an• we have come to this large conclusion. Were Mr. Ran•olph'a plan to be a•opte•, in no time at all the larger states woul• have the upper han• in both branches of the Congress. The states possessing a small population woul• have little power in the first house an• none in the secon•. Thus we coul• not possibly accept Mr. Ran•olph's plan.

On June 15th, William Paterson presented his now-famous New Jersey Plan.

We, of New Jersey, •o not feel the necessity of aban•oning the Articles of Confe•eration. We feel that with the proper revisions, the national government's power may be increase•. However, the government shoul• operate upon the states an• not in•ivi•ual citizens. We feel that Mr. Ran•olph's legislative plan is not to the best a•vantage of the people.

Our proposal calls for revision of the Articles of Confe•eration in such a way as to •estroy the evils now exerting their influence upon the people an• to have a Congress whereby all states, regar•less of population, woul• have equal representation. All •efen•e• their plans. James Ma•ison, a •elegate from Virginia who kept the minutes of that meeting, spoke out against the New Jersey Plan. He expressly refuse• to comply with a con-stitutional requisition of Congress an• yiel•e• no further (extracts from his speech in the convention against Paterson's plan).

I observe that the violators of the Fe•eral Articles have been numerous an• notorious. Among the most notorious was an act by New Jersey her-self, by which she expressly refuse• to comply with a constitutional requisition of Congress an• yiel•e• no further to the appeals of their •eputies, then barely rescin•e• her vote of refusal without passing any positive act of compliance.

I think it proper that the true nature of the existing confe•eracy shoul• be investigate•, an• I am not anxious to strengthen the foun•a-tions on which it now stan•s. Examine Mr. Ran•olph's plan an• say whether it promises satisfaction in two respects: first, to preserve the Union; secon•ly, to provi•e a government that will reme•y the evils felt by the states, both in their unite• an• in•ivi•ual capacities.

1. Will it prevent encroachments on the fe•eral authority? A ten•ency to such encroachments has been sufficiently exemplifie• among ourselves. By the Fe•eral Articles, trans-actions with the In•ians pertain to Congress, yet the states have entere• into treaties an• wars with them in several instances. In like manner, no two or more states can form any treaties among themselves without Congress's consent. Yet, Virginia, Marylan•, Pennsylvania, an• New Jersey have entere• into compacts without previous application or subsequent apology.

2. Will it prevent trespasses of the states on each other? Of these, enough has alrea•y been seen. Virginia an• Marylan• have given preference to their citizens in cases where the citizens of other states are entitle• to equal privileges by the Articles of Confe•eration. The emissions of paper money, an• other kin•re• measures, are also aggressions.

3. Will it secure the internal tranquillity of the states themselves? The insurrections in Massachusetts admonished all the conditions of the danger to which they were exposed.

4. Will it secure good internal legislation and administration to the particular states? In developing the evils of the political system of the United States, it is proper to take into view those which prevail within the states individually, as well as those which affect them collectively, since the former directly affects the whole.

5. I beg the smaller states, which are most attached to Mr. Paterson's plan to consider the situation it would leave you. First, you would continue to bear the expense of maintaining your delegates in Congress. It ought not to be said that no others have a right to complain if you are willing to bear this burden. As far as it leads the smaller states to forbear keeping up a representation by which the public business is delayed, it is evidently a matter of common concern. An examination of the minutes of Congress would satisfy everyone that this cause has frequently delayed public business and that the states most commonly underrepresented in Congress were not the larger states.

I remind the Convention of another consequence of leaving the burden of maintaining a representation in Congress to a small state. During a considerable period of the war, one of the representatives of Delaware, in whom alone, before the signing of the Confederation, the entire vote of the state, and after that event, one half of its vote, the frequently resided, was a citizen and *resi♦ent of Pennsylvania, an♦ hel♦ office in his own state incompatible with an appointment from it to Congress.*

During another perio♦, the same state was represente♦ by three ♦elegates, two of whom were citizens of Pennsylvania an♦ the thir♦ a citizen of New Jersey. These (♦elegates) must have been inten♦e♦ to avoi♦ the bur♦en of supporting ♦elegates from their own state. But whatever might have been the cause, was not, in effect, the vote of one State ♦ouble♦, an♦ the influence of another increase♦ by it?

Finally, a compromise was proposed and accepted.

By William Johnson and Roger Sherman from Connecticut, who addressed the convention.

Mr. Chairman, ♦istinguishe♦ ♦elegates, The Connecticut ♦elegation in♦ee♦ un♦erstan♦s the situation of the legislature which confronts us. Are we to go along with Mr. Ran♦olph's plan an♦ aban♦on the Articles, thus giving the new government more power, representing the states equally accor♦ing to the population? Or are we to si♦e with Mr. Paterson an♦ strengthen the Articles, giving the present government more power, representing the states equally regar♦less of population?

After pon♦ering upon this question for some time, we have formulate♦ a compromise that we are sure will satisfy both si♦es of the question. Our proposal is this: let the Congress consist of two houses in one of which representation shall be equal regar♦less of population. On the other let the representation be base♦ upon population.

> *This plan was adopted but there immediately arose the question of the representation of the slave population and slave trade traffic in America.*

The next question discussed was the most critical part of the convention. What are we to do about the issue of slavery? This would help determine the nature of the government being created. Were we to be a plutocracy, an oligarchy, a land-owning aristocracy, or a democracy? I don't think we have resolved that question. We never presented a plan to promote equality.

By Rufus King, from Massachusetts

The admission of slaves is a most grating circumstance to my mind, and I would not believe so to a great part of the people of America. In two great points, the hands of the legislature are absolutely tied. The importation of slaves cannot be prohibited. Exports cannot be taxed. Is this reasonable? What are the great objects of the general system?

First, defense against foreign invasion; secondly, against internal sedition shall one part of the United States be bound to defend another part, and that other part be at liberty, not only to increase its own that danger but to withhold the compensation for the burden?

If slaves are to be imported, shall not the exports produced by their labor supply a revenue the better to enable the general government to defend their masters? I had hoped that some accommodation would have taken place on this subject, that, at least, a time would have been limited for the importation of slaves.

I could never agree to let them be imported without limitation and then be represented in the national legislature. At all events shall be computed, either slaves should not be represented, or exports should be taxable?

By Gouverneur Morris, from Pennsylvania

I could never concur with upholding domestic slavery. It is a nefarious institution. It is the curse of heaven on the states where it prevails. Upon what principle is it that slaves shall be computed in the representation? Are they men? Then make them citizens and let them vote. Are they property? Why, then, is no other property included?

The houses in this city are worth more than all the wretched slaves who covered the rice swamps of South Carolina. The admission of slaves into the representation was fairly explained, comes to this – not the inhabitants of Georgia and South Carolina, who goes to the coast of Africa and ends in defiance of the most sacred laws of humanity; here's a way his fellow creatures from their dearest connections, and then them to the most cruel bondage, shall have more votes, in a government instituted for the protection of the rights of mankind, then this citizen of Pennsylvania or New Jersey.

And what is the proposed compensation to the northern states for a sacrifice of every principle of right or every impulse of humanity? They are to bind themselves to March, their militia or the defense of the Southern States, for their defense against these very slaves they complain about. On the other hand, the southern states are not to be restrained from importing fresh supplies of wretched Africans at once to increase the danger of attack and the difficulty of the fence.

Let us idle to suppose that the general government can stretch its hand directly and only do it through the medium of exports, imports, and exercises. For what, they are all the sacrifices to be made? I would sooner *submit myself to a tax for paying for all the Negroes in the Unite• States than sa••le posterity with such a constitution.*

At length, it was agreed that every five slaves should now be counted as three White free men.

By **Luther Martin,** from Maryland

I propose to vary article 7, section 4 to allow the prohibition of the tax on the importation of slaves to allow the prohibition of the slave tra•e. In the first place, as five slaves are to be counte• as three free men in the apportionment of representatives, such a clause woul• leave an encouragement to this traffic. In the secon• place, slaves weaken one part of the Union, which the other parts are boun• to protect; the privilege of importing them is therefore unreasonable. The thir• place, it is inconsistent with the principles of an•, in the revolution, an• •ishonorable to the American character to have such a feature in the Constitution.

By **John Rutledge,** from South Carolina

I fail to see how the importation of slaves can be encourage• by this section. I am not apprehensive of insurrections an• woul• rea•ily exempt the other states from the obligation to protect the Southern States against them. Religion an• humanity have nothing to •o with this question. Interest alone is the governing principle with nations. The true question is whether the Southern States shall or shall not be parties to the Union. If the Northern States consult their interest, they woul• not oppose the increase of slaves, increasing the commo•ities they woul• become the carriers of.

By **Oliver Ellsworth,** from Connecticut

I am for leaving the clause as it stands. Let every state import what it pleases. The morality or wisdom of slavery are considerations belonging to the states themselves. That which enriches a part enriches the whole, and the states are the best judges of their particular interests. The old Confederation did not meddle with this point, and I do not see any greater necessity for bringing it within the policy of the new one.

By Charles Cotesworth Pinckney, from South Carolina

I can never receive the plan if it prohibits the slave trade. In every proposed extension of the powers of Congress, South Carolina has expression; and watchfully excepted that of meddling with the importation of negroes. If the states are all left at liberty on this subject, South Carolina may perhaps by degrees, do of herself what is wished, as Virginia and Maryland already have done.

By Roger Sherman, from Connecticut

I am for leaving the clause as it stands. I disapprove of the slave trade, yet as the states are now possessed of the right to import slaves, as the public good does not require it to be taken from them, and as it is expedient to have as few objections as possible to the proposed scheme of government. I think it best to leave the matter as we find it. I observe that the abolition of slavery seems to be going on in the U.S. and that the good sense of the several states will probably, by degrees, complete it. I urge on the Convention the necessity of dispatching its business.

By George Mason, from Virginia

The evil of having slaves was experienced during the late war. This infernal traffic originated in the avarice of British merchants. The British government constantly checked the attempts of Virginia to put a stop to it. *The whole question concerns not the importing States alone but the entire Union.*

Enslave• people have been treate• as they might have been by the enemy; they woul• have prove• •angerous instruments in their han•s. But their folly was •ealt with by the slaves as it •i• by the Tories. Marylan• an• Virginia have alrea•y prohibite• the importation of slaves expressly; North Carolina has •one the same in substance...From every point of view, I hel• it essential that the general government have the power to prevent the increase of slavery.

By Oliver Ellsworth, from Connecticut

As I have never owne• a slave, I coul• not ju•ge the effects of slavery on character. However, if it is to be consi•ere• in a moral light, we ought to go further an• free those alrea•y in the country. As slaves also multiply so fast in Virginia an• Marylan• that it is cheaper to raise than import them, whilst in the sickly rice swamps, foreign supplies are necessary; if we go no further than is urge•, we shall be unjust towar•s South Carolina an• Georgia.

Let us not interme••le. As the population increases, poor laborers will be plenty to ren•er slaves useless. Slavery, in time, will not be a speck in our country. Provision is alrea•y ma•e in Connecticut for abolishing it. An• the abolition has alrea•y taken place in Massachusetts. The •anger of foreign influence insurrections will become a motive for the kin• treatment of the slaves.

By Charles Cotesworth Pinckney, from South Carolina

It is my firm opinion that if all my colleagues an• I were to sign the Constitution an• use our personal influence, it woul• be of no avail in obtaining the assent of our constituents. So as well as North Carolina and Georgia cannot do without slaves. As to Virginia, she will gain by stopping the importations.

Her slaves will rise in value, and she has more than she wants. It would be unequal to require South Carolina and Georgia to confederate on such unequal terms. I contend that the importation of slaves would be for the carrying trade; the more consumption also; and the more of this, the more revenue of the common treasury. I think it reasonable that slaves should be dutied like other exports but should consider a rejection of the clause as an exclusion of South Carolina from the Union.

By Abraham Baldwin, from Georgia

I had conceived national objects alone to be before the Convention, not such as, like the present, were local. Georgia is decided on this point. That state has always hitherto supposed a general government to be the pursuit of the central states, who wished to have a vortex for everything, that her distance would preclude her from equal advantage, and that she could not purchase it by yielding national powers.

From this, it might be understood in what light she views an attempt to abridge one of her favorite prerogatives. If left to herself, she may probably put a stop to the evil.

By James Wilson, from Pennsylvania

If South Carolina and Georgia were themselves disposed to get rid of the importation of slaves in a short time, as has been suggested, they would never refuse to Unite because the importation might be prohibited. As this section now stands, all articles imported are to be taxed. Slaves alone are exempt. This is, in fact, a bounty on that article.

By Elbridge Gerry, from Massachusetts

We have nothing to ∎o with the con∎uct of the states as to slaves, but ought to be careful not to give any sanction to it.

By John Dickinson, from Delaware

On every principle of honor an∎ safety, I consi∎er it ina∎missible that the importation of slaves shoul∎ be authorize∎ to the states by The Constitution. The true question is whether the importation woul∎ promote or impe∎e national happiness. I ∎o not believe that the Southern States woul∎ refuse to confe∎erate on the account apprehen∎e∎, especially as the general government's power is not likely to be imme∎iately exercise∎.

By Rufus King, from Massachusetts

I think the subject shoul∎ be consi∎ere∎ in a political light only. If two states ∎o not agree to the Constitution, as states on one si∎e, I cannot affirm with equal belief that great an∎ equal opposition woul∎ be experience∎ from the other states.

By John Langdon, from New Hampshire

I am for giving the power to the general government. I coul∎ not, with goo∎ conscience, leave it with the states, who coul∎ then go on with the traffic, without being restraine∎ by the opinions here given, that they will themselves cease to import slaves.

By General Charles Cotesworth Pinckney, from South Carolina

I ∎o not think South Carolina woul∎ stop her importations of slaves in any short time, but only stop them occasionally, as she now ∎oes. Slaves might be liable to an equal tax with other imports, which I think is right an• woul• remove one •ifficulty that ha• been starte•.

By **John Rutledge,** from South Carolina

The expectation is vain if the Convention thinks that North Carolina, South Carolina, an• Georgia will ever agree to the plan unless their right to import slaves be untouche•. The people of those states will never be such fools as to give up such an important interest. Section 4 of article 7 shoul• not be taken out.

By **Gouverneur Morris,** from Pennsylvania

I think the whole subject shoul• be committe• to a navigation act, inclu•ing the clauses relating to taxes on exports. These things may form a bargaining groun• among the Northern an• Southern States.

By **Pierce Butler**, from South Carolina

I shall never agree to the power of taxing exports.

By **Roger Sherman**, from Connecticut

Let the Southern States import slaves is better than to part with them. I am oppose• to a tax on slaves as property. I acknowle•ge the fact that if the power of prohibiting importation was given to the general government, it woul• be exercise•. It woul• be its •uty to exercise power.

By **Edmund Randolph**, from Virginia

I am for committing so that some mi••le groun• might, if possible, be foun•. I coul• never agree to the clause as it stan•s;

I woul• sooner risk the Constitution. If agreeing to the clause, it woul• revolt the Quakers, the Metho•ists, an• many others in the states having no slaves. On the other han•, two states might be lost to the Union. Let us then try the chance of a commitment.

At length, the Constitution was finished. All that remained was for the delegates to put their signatures on the document.

*Disclaimer: What you have read are the actual words spoken at the Constitutional Convention in 1787. The author notes that no opinions were added, and no positions were taken. What appears on these pages are the thoughts of these men from the 18th century. Some did not speak during the entire convention, and some did not even vote for or against the propositions. In the end, the door was open, they walked out, resumed their lives, and most of them never saw each other again.

*A vote was taken, and as a result, the whole subject was committed to a navigation act. Thus the question of the slave trade was settled but by no means resolved or abolished.

Another problem confronting the delegates was the election of the President. If Congress were to elect the President, he might be fearful of doing anything against their wishes. However, the delegates were not confident about the people choosing the President. So a compromise was worked out. Each state was to have a certain number of electors, which would be determined by the total number of senators and representatives. If there were a tie, the House of Representatives would make the final decision.

Thirty-four years later came the first attempt to provide a second chance for our nation. This came about in 1821, and it happened in the state of New York.

> Since the whole course of political evolution in other advanced democracies has been in the direction of responsible and efficient executive leadership, and since substantial gains in American government have come from halting steps in that direction, the Constitutional Convention is called upon to answer this fundamental question: "Is it desirable to retain a system of government that secures only irresponsible and invisible leadership, or should cognizance be taken of the expedients which have been developed during the last hundred years for making leadership effective and responsible to the people."

The purpose of the 1787 convention was to establish a government that would secure the rights and liberties of all Americans. People were looking for more significant expansion and greater detail in what promises were made, and they were expecting greater specificity through the means chosen to achieve those goals. Caldwell acknowledged with gratitude the beneficence of God in permitting us to make choices and, by doing so, expand the specified freedoms in greater detail.

The rise of partisan politics arose, and it wasn't pretty. The Federalist Party seemed to make it clear that the people's wishes were not to become their priority. Governor Clinton clarified that whatever was best for furthering the party's agenda was foremost. Self-interest raised its ugly head. The population had quadrupled, but 80% of that gain came from land stolen from the Iroquois. The ordinary citizens were restless and wanted change. They leaned toward democratic views and supported them. This was not a happy time.

The 1787 Constitution met the needs of the freeholders within the Hudson Valley, but the farmers of the western inland counties were left out and restless about not getting "a seat at the table."The renters and tenant farmers were not happy, and the insistent demand for universal manhood suffrage grew. Class lines were sharply drawn. The people's needs were not being met.

John Jay said, "Those who own the country ought to govern it." The new generation, the young, had their opinion; they believed that since they helped produce, improve and preserve property, they should have a voice in their government, equal to those who owned it!

Dewitt Clinton published the *Statesman*, a newspaper of prominence, and Daniel Tompkins began publishing the *Argus*. The democrats started by saying that society was not a money partnership but an association of all men to promote the common good. Clinton's supporters disagreed. The lines were drawn.

Many people were alarmed by the idea of universal suffrage. Some saw the benefits of including all, but many held to the left to the ever-expanding middle class left their beliefs and were alarmed by the desire of some just to allow everyone to vote. J.D. Hammond took a midway position. This was the road taken, and it was soon left in the middle class's lap to decide.

Property qualifications were removed for Whites, but the qualifications remained high for Blacks. It was prejudiced and obvious, but why was that the case? The capabilities of Blacks were these. A Black man had to be a state citizen for three years and one year preceding any election and own a freehold estate worth $250 free and clear, upon which he had been rated and taxed.

As compensation for being denied suffrage, Blacks were not subject to taxation unless they were allowed to vote. This passed for freedom then, but it was not uniform in every locality. Some Whites wanted to exclude other Whites whom they referred to as "depraved."

What was beginning was a feeling that the people themselves were becoming the most significant motivating force in our democracy. That was the feeling then, and it remains intact today. Those led the overarching change that began with courage, who found time to speak and participate with their neighbors and others with whom they would meet and share thoughts.

This Constitution, which the voters approved on January 15th, 16th, and 17th of 1822, was the first revision of the 1787 product produced in secret. It was more open and democratic but didn't move the needle. We still have a long road to travel. Who would pick up the flag and lead the way?

7

The Aftermath of the Constitutional Convention

"I can't imagine a person becoming
a success who doesn't give the game
everything he's got all."
– Walter Cronkite.

In many history books, the conclusion or the aftermath of the Constitutional Convention is never discussed. I'm sure the majority of the American population could not recall that something was left to be challenged.

At the Convention, the delegates were not comfortable or confident about the people choosing the president. These people, they opined, felt that the common man's lack of education limited his intelligence, so his judgment couldn't even be trusted. After the Declaration of Independence of 1776, with its ideals about equality, how could we now discriminate between people? How could they even consider giving different groups different rights, access to information, and voting?

Gouveneur Morris offered that if the Blacks imported (or kidnapped) are now subject to human bondage, are they now without the protection of the rights of mankind? He thought, "We should leave the matter as we found it and that in time, the good states will probably, by degrees, complete it." Some delegates did so, while others did not wish to support the paper. Like Roger Sherman disapproved of White men owning enslaved Black people, others believed that the Constitution should be approved, leaving the question unresolved.

Several delegates gave reasons why they did or did not sign their names: C Pinckney, Mr. Gerry, Benjamin Franklin, H Gorham, R. King, and D.Carroll, G. Washington, E. Randolph, Gouverneur Morris, H. Williamson, A. Hamilton, W. Blount, J. Ingersoll, J. Wilson, Ellsworth, and Sherman.

The transcript of their statements follows:

By Charles Pinckney, from South Carolina

Nothing but confusion an● contrariety will spring from this experiment. The states will never agree on their plans, an● the ●eputies to a secon● Convention, coming together un●er the ●iscor●ant impressions of their constituents, will never agree. Conventions are serious things an● ought not to be repeale●. I object to the contemptible weakness an● ●epen●ence of the executive. I object to the power of a majority, only, of Congress, over commerce. But, apprehen●ing the ●anger of general confusion an• an ultimate •ecision by the wor•, I shall give the plan my support.

By Elbridge Gerry, from Massachusetts

I woul• like to state the objection that forces me to withhol• my name from the Constitution.

1. The •uration an• reliability of the Senate.

2. The power of the House of Representatives to conceal the journals of Congress over the places of election [voting rights].

3. The power of Congress over the places of election

4. The unlimite• power of Congress over their compensation.

5. That Massachusetts has not a •ue share of representatives allotte• to her.

6. That three-fifths of the Blacks are to be represente• as if they were free men.

7. That un•er the power over commerce, monopolies may be establishe•.

8. The Vice-Presi•ent being ma•e hea• of the Senate. I coul•, however, get over all these if the rights of the citizens were not ren•ere• insecure-first by the general power of the legislature to; raise armies an• money without limit an• to make what laws they may please to call necessary an• proper.

By Benjamin Franklin, from Pennsylvania

Mr. Presi•ent: I confess that there are several parts of this Constitution which I •o not at present approve, but I am not sure I shall never approve them. Having live• long, I have experience• many instances of being oblige•, by better information or fuller consi•eration, to change opinions, even on important subjects I once thought right but found otherwise.

Therefore, as I grow, I am more apt to doubt my judgment and the judgment of others. Most men, indeed, as well as most sects in religion, think themselves in possession of all truth and that wherever others differ from them, it is so far in these sentiments, agree to this Constitution, with all of its faults, if they are such; because I think a general government necessary for us, and there is no form of government, but what may be a blessing to the people if well administered; and believe further, that this is likely to be well issued for years, and can only end in despotism, as other forms have done before it, when the people shall become so corrupted as to need despotic government, being incapable of any other.

I doubt, too, whether any other Convention we can obtain may be able to make a better Constitution. For when you assemble a number of men to have the advantage of their joint wisdom, you inevitably assemble with those men all their prejudices, their passions, their errors of opinion, their local love interests; therefore, astonish me, sir, to find this system approaching so near to perfection as it does; and I think it will astonish our enemies, who are waiting with confidence to hear that our councils are confounded, like those of the builders of Babel; and that our states are on the point of separation, only to meet hereafter for the purpose of cutting one another's throats.

Thus I consent, sir, to this Constitution because I expect no better and am not sure that it is not the best; I sacrifice my opinions of its errors for the public good. I have never whispered a syllable of them abroad. Within these walls, they were born, and here they shall die.

Suppose every one of us, in returning to our constituents, were to report the objections he has had to it and endeavor to gain partisans in support of them.

In that case, we might prevent it's being generally received and thereby lose all the salutary effects and significant advantages resulting naturally in our favor among foreign nations, as well as among ourselves, from our actual or apparent unanimity. Much of the strength and efficiency of any government in procuring and securing happiness for the people depends on the general opinion of the goodness of the government and the wisdom and integrity of its governors.

I hope, therefore, that for our sakes, as part of the People, and for the sake of posterity, we shall act heartily and unanimously in recommending this Constitution (if approved by Congress and confirmed by the conventions) wherever our influence may extend and turn our future thoughts - and endeavors to the means of having it well administered, on the whole, sir, I cannot help expressing a wish that every member of the Convention, who may still have objections to it, would with me, on this occasion, doubt a little of his infallibility, and to make manifest our unanimity, put his name to this instrument.

I move that the members sign the Constitution and offer the following as a convenient form; done in Convention by the unanimous consent of the States present, the 17th of September, etc. In witness whereof, we have hereunto subscribed our names.

By Nathaniel Gorham, from Massachusetts

If it is not too late, I would wish, to lessen objection to the Constitution, that the clause declaring that "the number of representatives shall not exceed one for every forty thousand," which has produced so much *iscussion, might be yet reconsi*ere*, to strike out "forty thousan*," an* insert "thirty thousan*." This woul* not establish that as an absolute rule but only give Congress a great latitu*e, which coul* not be thought unreasonable.

By Rufus King, from Massachusetts, and Daniel Carroll, from Maryland

We secon* an* support the i*eas of Mr. Gorham.

By George Washington, from Virginia

Although my situation has hitherto restraine* me from offering my sentiments on questions *epen*ing in the House, an*, it might be thought, that ought now to impose silence on me. Yet, I coul* not forbear expressing my wish that the alteration propose* might take place. It is much to be *esire* that the objections to the plan recommen*e* might be ma*e as few as possible.

The smallness of the proportion of representatives has rights an* interests of the people. I acknowle*ge that it has always appeare* among the exceptionable parts of the plan, an*, late as the present moment is for a*mitting amen*ments, I think this is of so much consequence that it woul* give me satisfaction to see it a*opte*.

No opposition was ma*e to the proposition of Mr. Gorham, an* it was agree* to unanimously.

By Edmund Randolph, from Virginia

I must refuse to sign the Constitution, notwithstan*ing the vast majority an* venerable names that woul* sanction its wis*om an* worth. However, I *o not mean by this refusal that I shoul* oppose the Constitution without doors. I mean only to keep myself free to be governed by my duty; my future judgment should prescribe intent.

I refuse to sign because the object of the Convention will be just to ratify the plan, and confusion must ensue. With such a view of the subject, I ought not, I could not, by pledging myself to support the plan, restrain myself from taking such steps as might appear to be most consistent with the public good.

By Gouverneur Morris, from Pennsylvania

I, too, have objections, but, considering the present plan as the best that is to be attained, I shall take it with all its faults. The majority had determined in its favor, and by that determination, I shall abide. The moment this plan goes forth, all other considerations will be laid aside, and the great question will be, shall there be a national government or not? And this must take place, or a general anarchy will be the alternative.

By Hugh Williamson, from North Carolina

I suggest that the signing should be confined to the letter accompanying the Constitution to Congress, which might perhaps do nearly as well, and would be found satisfactory to some members who dislike the Constitution, do not think a better plan is to be expected, and I have no scruples against putting my name to it.

By Alexander Hamilton, from New York

A few characters of consequence, by opposing, or even refusing to sign the Constitution, might make infinite mischief by kindling the latent spark that lurks under an enthusiasm in favor of the Convention, which *may soon subsi•e. No man's i•eas are more remote from the plan than my own are known to be, but is it possible to •eliberate between anarchy, an• convulsion, on one si•e an• the chance of goo• to be expecte• from the plan on the other?*

By **William Blount,** by North Carolina

I will not sign to ple•ge myself in support of the plan, but I am relieve• by the form propose• an• will, without committing myself, attest to the fact that the plan is the unanimous act of the states in the Convention.

By **Benjamin Franklin,** from Pennsylvania

From what Mr. Ran•olph has sai•, I thought myself allu•e• to in the remarks offere• this morning to the House. When •rawing up that paper, I •i• not know that any particular member woul• refuse to sign his name to the instrument an• hope to be so un•erstoo•. I possess a high sense of obligation to Mr. Ran•olph for having brought forwar• the plan in the first instance an• for the assistance he has given in its progress; an• I hope that he will yet lay asi•e his objections an•, by concurring with his brethren, prevent the great mischief which the refusal of his name might pro•uce.

By **Edmund Randolph,** from Virginia

I cannot but regar• the signing in the propose• form as the same as signing the Constitution. The change of form, therefore, can make no •ifference to me. I repeat that, in refusing to sign the Constitution, I take a step that might be the most awful of my life; but it is •ictate• by my conscience, an• it is not possible for me to hesitate—much less to change.

By Elbridge Gerry, from Massachusetts

Whilst the plan was depending, I treated it with all the freedom I thought it deserved. I now feel myself bound, as I am disposed, to treat it with respect due to the act of the Convention. I hope I shall not violate that respect in declaring, on this occasion, my fears that a civil war may result from the present crisis in the United States.

In Massachusetts, particularly, I see the danger of this catastrophic event. In what state there are two parties, one devoted to democracy - the worse, I think, of all political evils; the other as violent in the opposite extreme. From the collision of these, in opposing and resisting the Constitution, confusion is great to be feared.

I think it necessary, for this and other reasons, that the plan should have been proposed in a more mediating way in order to abate the heat and opposition of parties. As has been passed by the Convention, I was persuaded it would have a contrary effect. I cannot, therefore, by signing the Constitution, pledge myself to abide by it at all events. The proposed form makes no difference with me. But if it was not otherwise apparent, the refusals to sign should never be known from me.

By Charles Pinckney, from South Carolina

We are not likely to gain many converts by the ambiguity of the proposed form of signing. I think it best to be candid and let the form speak the substance. I will sign the Constitution with a view to support it with all my influence and wish to pledge myself accordingly.

By Benjamin Franklin, from Pennsylvania

It is too soon to pledge ourselves before Congress, and our Constituents shall have approved the plan.

By Jarod Ingersoll, from Pennsylvania

I ●o not consi●er the signing, either as a mere attestation of the fact or as ple●ging the signers to support the Constitution at all events, but as a recommen●ation of what, all things consi●ere●, was the most eligible.

By Rufus King, from Massachusetts

I suggest that the Journals of the Convention shoul● be either ●estroye● or ●eposite● in the custo●y of the presi●ent. I think, if they suffere● from being ma●e public, a ba● use woul● be ma●e of them by those who woul● wish to prevent the a●option of the Constitution!

By James Wilson, from Pennsylvania

I prefer the secon● expe●ient. I ha● at one time like● it the best! But as false suggestions may be propagate●, it shoul● not be ma●e impossible to contra●ict them.

A question was then put on the floor about ●epositing the journals, an● other papers of the Convention, in the han●s of the presi●ent. Only one state, Marylan●, was oppose● to this.

The members then procee●e● to sign the Constitution, as finally amen●e●. The Constitution was signe● by all the members except Mr. Ran●olph, Mr. Mason, an● Mr. Gerry, who ●ecline● to give it the sanction of their names.

The Convention dissolved itself by an adjournment.

Here are the following comments that were made by those remaining in the hall.

By Rufus King, from Massachusetts

*The importation of enslave• people coul• not be prohibite• or taxe•! If
slaves are importe•, Shall not the exports pro•uce• by their labor provi•e
a revenue the better to enable the general government to •efen• the
Masters of those slaves But, the slaves shoul• not be represente•, or
exports shoul• be taxable?*

By Gouverneur Morris, from Pennsylvania

*I coul• never concur with the i•ea of supporting slavery in the
colonies. Slavery is Nefarious. How can slavery be counte• in representa-
tions? Are slaves to be consi•ere• as men? Woul• that enable them to be
consi•ere• Citizens? Will these slaves be permitte• to vote? Aren't they
property?*

*What if the slave owner who travels to Africa returns to our Shores
with more Blacks in •efiance of our most sacre• laws of humanity? What
if bringing more slaves here an• one •ay those slaves outnumber us? Who
thought of that? What if these slaves outnumber us? What if a large
number of slaves increases the •anger to us all! I woul• sooner sa••le
myself with the tax for paying for all the Blacks in these Unite• States
than sa••le posterity with such a Constitution. How can we harbor in our
Constitution the concept that the continue• importation of Slaves is inconsistent or •ishonorable within the scope of our Constitution?*

By John Rutledge, from South Carolina

*I fail to un•erstan• how the importation of slaves is encourage• by
this rationale.*

By Oliver Ellsworth, from Connecticut

Let every state import what pleases it. The morality or wisdom of slavery are considerations belonging to each state. The stakes are the best judges of their particular interests. The Articles did not meddle with this point, and I do not see any necessity for bringing this concept within the policy of the new one.

By Charles Pinckney, from South Carolina

I cannot support this plan if it prohibits the slave trade!

By Roger Sherman, from Connecticut

I disapprove of the slave trade, but the states have the right to import enslaved people.

By Oliver Ellsworth, from Connecticut

I do not own a slave, and I disapprove of the practice of slavery. We should free those already in the country. Slavery, in time, will not be a speck in our country's history! As the population increases, poor laborers will be plenty, so many enslaved people will be useless!

*Disclaimer: Most people were unaware of what had transpired during the Constitutional Convention. They had not even been asked to participate! Keep in mind that at the time of the 1787 Convention, there were 1,100,000 White Americans and 800,000 enslaved Black people and that the participants at the Philadelphia convention were limited to 55 White men. These 55 attendees were *cherry-picked.* The people in America had to go along with all of it; This was a poor start for what was to become a young democracy.

Those in power sought to *pull the wool over the eyes* of the American citizenry. They believed that they could do this by themselves simply by restricting the people from participating in what was happening. This was not a democracy; it began as a plutocracy —limited to rich land-owning men and their friends.

Less than 25% of our country's residents were the only ones who thought they had an entitlement. They believed we would remain that *beacon on a hill* and become the world's envy.

At no time did anyone believe that all of us were entitled to human rights in the 18th century! How has that changed?

Part of the conclusion of the Convention included a speech by Hugh Williamson of North Carolina, who said, "I do not think a better plan is to be expected, and I have no scruples against putting my name to it!" Try defending that thinking today.

There was absolutely no thought given to what would be the opinions of Americans of the future who would have to live with the consequences of these events. Perhaps, they considered what Americans thought in the future was not an issue — what a travesty!

We must consider indifference, and we must annihilate it.

8

Seeking Equality

> "I have never been hurt by any-
> thing I didn't say."
> – Calvin Coolidge

It had been nearly three years since the convention in Philadelphia. On February 11th, 1790, two delegations of Quakers, one
from New York and the other from Pennsylvania, presented
petitions to the House of Representatives calling for the government to end the African slave trade.

The following day, on February 12th, 1790, it became apparent
that the Constitution would not have been approved at the
convention because many Whites believed that Blacks were not
considered equal to the White majority.

Therefore, despite the concept of equality introduced by the
Declaration of Independence of 1776 and the ratification of the
Constitution, As discussed in chapter 5 and summarized here,
which included the Three-Fifths Compromise. That compromise

disputed *equality* when it betrayed the ideals enunciated in our Preamble. This started this nation on the wrong foot.

This new nation was teetering. It was teetering because *equality* was only a word in the Constitution. This teetering was simply ignored. Ideals were to remain only as ideals, not even goals! What existed in America was not equality. Neglected but not forgotten for over two centuries. The American people were asleep at the wheel.

The Federal government could not tamper and could not even discuss stopping the slave trade until after 1808. The American people were asleep at the switch. Bringing up the subject of equality was itself a time bomb. The entire discussion could not take place. Hundreds of thousands of lives were involved.

Tens of thousands of families were affected. Americans were all told to just *eal with it.* This was not even in the neighborhood of *equality.* How could this problem be dealt with if it couldn't be discussed? The 1787 Constitution prohibited any deliberative body from discussing slavery and all of the lives held in limbo until 1808, but that was two decades in the future.

What did the word equality mean as written in the Constitution? What did the phrase equality mean to women? How would this nation survive? Two centuries later, this subject still has yet to be dealt with. Still, that question is worse than that unanswered question between Blacks and White Americans would remain in place because these White Americans didn't want to talk about the conditions of everyone. They only thought about themselves.

Black Americans were not given any options. They just had to go along with whatever happened and whatever others decided. Black Americans just had to do what the Whites thrived on because they were in charge. Life would just go on for the White

Americans, and everyone would have to deal with this situation as it was.

The government was expanded, and people, Whites, and Blacks, had children and expanded their families, but the Blacks had to settle for the perpetuation of what existed. They had a minor role, while Whites got the lion's share of the wealth.

The Blacks were not entitled because they were not White. Nothing was promised to them. The Preamble to the Constitution had pledged to another generation that when you came around the corner to find what had been promised, another promise remained unfulfilled.

The gulf between the landowners, the farmers, and everyone else would get more expansive, and the Preamble of the Constitution's goals would become increasingly more remote. The promises of equality in land ownership were allowed quietly to slip away.

That was the plan, and no one was talking about it. Some in government quietly talked about this inhumane treatment. Still, they did not want to rouse the slave owners or create apprehension that the national government would soon alert everyone that slavery would be abolished in all states. They just let the subject be dropped.

These were human lives, American lives, but it was turning into a nightmarish situation because no one could come to the discussion with anything new to say or with any clues on how to avoid this impasse.

Virginia took the position that the national government could not do anything about the solution to this problem because it was a state matter, and the people of Virginia thought this remained a state's rights issue. George Mason believed that the states had more authority to extend the slave trade.

Since slavery was sanctioned by the Old Testament and was accepted as a long-term custom among African civilizations, this became the precedent. Since slavery was established long before 1619 and continued through the writing of The Constitution, it didn't have to adhere to any changes sought in 1790.

It was a split world. People were living the example of "do what I say and not what I do," but words matter. Words have significance and meaning, and they must match your actions. The Constitution should have meant something and should have been binding on everyone.

Later, words uttered by Thomas Jefferson, who was then our Secretary of State, appeared in notes on the state of Virginia. The recorded notes raised the question of *what woul. be .one with the enslave. people after being free.*.

Jefferson had said that the two races could not be brought together on an equal basis because of long-established prejudices involved in mixing the races. Many people in America still do not provide or believe in that equality. America, you must live by the words that govern us. These words can offer freedom and hope to all, but they fell short then, and they fall short now.

While we accepted new citizens into this country as long as they had a certain look, all who came here were soon shuffled into a category of free or enslaved. So at that time, we honestly did not offer freedom to all on an equal basis. We do not even promise it to our unborn. Perhaps we have this because even freedom is sometimes overrated!

Great Britain had eight million residents in 1775, and the thirteen colonies had about 2.5 million people and half a million slaves. With Brittan having a larger population, they had the more prominent voice and say in the political pull at that time.

In 1774 and 1775, John Adams and Thomas Jefferson both had articles published, in the same magazines, stating their opinions of the political goings-on regarding what England was doing and how they were not listening to the colonists. Adams and Jefferson felt it was time that other colonies got involved within the parameters of that discussion to be represented so that taxation could be fair.

Leaders are expected to be the servants of the people and managers of the people. The phrase *no taxation without representation* arose from that and was heard in many places in America. So, it should be accepted that the Declaratory Act of 1765, enacted by Britain's Parliament, which was binding on the colonies, was not justified because the colonists were not participants in the promulgation of the laws.

Jefferson said in his summary of the rights of British America published in 1774 that the plan "was to provide a path so that his brethren could protest the language coming from the English Parliament regarding what the colonists were doing."

When the tumult started to grow because of the boldness he exhibited, there was growing clamor for Jefferson to take the lead to present the case for the colonies and the issue of what would become of lands that would one day become Texas.

Inclusive of this, he felt that the colonies had to face Britain's overbearing attitude and that Jefferson should draft that position. Therefore, those words (credited to Jefferson from the Preamble to the Declaration of Independence written by Ben Franklin) were recognized as the bedrock that would unite the population.

In January of 1775, Adams decided that he had to respond. Adams had arrived at opposition within a framework that demonstrated loyalty to the crown. He stated, "I'm not for a new Constitution."

On his way back from England, Jefferson heard that Britain, under King George III, wanted to eliminate slavery. This was going to start an underpinning current that slavery is immoral and that if a place like America believed in its ideals, it had declared in the Declaration of Independence, then it must reflect that. Jefferson added the phrase "all men are created equal."

Adding to this insult is the question of the purpose of the imposition of slavery on the American colonies. Was it tradition? Was it just the way it was? No, the colonies did not request slavery, yet it was here for over 100 years. Colonists and enslaved people had no say. In this position, there was no path for the colonists to exclude any further importations of these permanently indentured and uneducated souls.

Voting did not even enter the discussion if the colonists wanted to keep or abolish slavery. Allowing the people, every man, and woman, to have a vote about the method of participation was not even discussed. The foundation for voting then was based upon the ownership of property. Your vote would not have counted if you had no property and were an indentured servant or enslaved person. (And obviously, women and slaves couldn't own property, so they were excluded.)

Suppose Britain didn't care to add inclusivity to the equation back then. The colonists did not address the issue, giving each resident a path to participate in their country. This exclusion of the common man by the land-owning men was pervasive. The concept of change was not on anyone's lips or minds. So without a conception of change, the idea of full liberty or equality could not be introduced.

The very bedrock of the British constitution was that Britain was an Empire of laws and not of man. The elite ruled, and everyone else was subjected to what the elite wanted. The land-owning men, having emigrated from Europe, where they were accustomed to being the ruling elite, intended to keep their power. King George III most often had an opinion of his own, and he rarely withheld his voice, thus polluting the political waters of Britain, and that seeped over to the Americas.

But the colonists had been on their own for long enough to have established some rules and laws that the King could not enforce without starting a war. The colonists demanded that their voices be heard. They demanded freedom. The extra taxation on the people was a huge tipping point for America.

If you think about this from the elitists who have always had power, the idea of losing your strength and power is terrifying. Therefore you will rule with more regulations and restraints. This, however, has the opposite effect. People will rebel if they have tasted freedom and are forced to give it up.

The evolution from the sharing of opinions by elitists to now hearing and involving the masses was frightening to fathom. This was the proposal of the colonists. They demanded to be heard, but that would mean allowing the majority to rule instead of just a select few. Again, if you have held power for centuries, sharing that power with people you judge as inferior to you is beyond comprehension.

In earlier times, imperfect humans needed robust laws to govern, they were subjected in thought and heart to the crown, such as the early colonists before the Declaration. After over 150 years of living distantly in the American colonies, where the immediate actions of the English King were not felt, the seeds of freedom and equality began to germinate. The colonists wanted freedom. We will see how they get it.

Getting a majority to lead the way and make decisions to bene-fit that majority has never been maintained up to this point. That is what a democracy is supposed to create for itself for each generation— a republican form of government that is responsive to the will of the majority.

But as a lasting note, someone smarter than me once said, "Every form of government allows people to suffer when the government is entrusted to a few."

It was time to make a change, but would America recognize and give this freedom to all if they won? Well, time would tell.

9

Mary Murray - The Heroine

"No country can ever truly flourish if it
stifles the potential of its women and
deprives itself of the contributions of half
of its citizens."-Michelle Obama

I have already taken you through the Constitutional Convention, and I did that to get to the heart of the matter of our country.
Now, to talk and share a story is called history. History, to some,
might feel repetitive or boring, but if we do not teach our real
history, we will be doomed to perpetuate what we think is the
truth but isn't.

I'll share a story about the American Revolution. Mary Murray
was awarded the Pewter Medallion. An inscription on the back
stated: "After the British captured Manhattan, she delayed the
enemy officers at her home. Her clever diversion permitted

American troops to escape." Who is this "she?" Her name was Mary Lindley Murray.

Again, a little history. Mary Lindley, born in 1726, was the daughter of Thomas Lindley, a Quaker and Blacksmith who had arrived in Philadelphia from Ireland in 1719. In 1727, with a group of other Quakers, including some of the most prominent merchants of the colony, Thomas Lindley became a founding owner of the Durham Furnace. He developed a great forge working this 6000-acre iron ore site on the Delaware River in Bucks County, Pennsylvania. It became one of the leading forces in the colonies.

Mary Lindley came from money, and now, as a youth, she met Robert Murray, a local merchant who lived a few miles away. After courting for a short period and they came to love each other. Originally a Presbyterian, Robert became a Quaker when they were married in 1744. After their marriage, Robert and Mary moved to Swatara, and their son Lindley Murray was born the following year.

I state this to show that this family had influence and power in the colonies. From 1745, Robert Murray operated as a merchant and made trading visits to the West Indies. These early trading efforts undoubtedly capitalized on his position as a miller of wheat and flour, which were products of Pennsylvania's significant exports to the West Indies. They traded those products for others and then shipped them back to New York.

The couple moved to New York City in 1753 after a short residence in North Carolina. Robert Murray quickly became one of the city's most successful and wealthiest merchants and influential figures. By this time, their oldest son, Lindley Murray, grew to young manhood and lived in New York.

It's important to note that Mary's husband had risen to wealth and power, and so did she. She would share in that new life as a wife but not as an individual because she was a woman. She could not hold property as a woman, but she shared that great fortune as a married woman.

In 1762, Robert rented land from the city of New York and built an estate named Inclenberg. That is Dutch for the *beautiful hill*. The land he rented, just over 29 acres, was located in what would become Manhattan's Murray Hill section.

Mary's home, Inclenberg, had front windows that commanded a view of Kip's Bay and the East River. The two-story great house was located at Park Avenue and 36th Street. Grand Central Station stands on what was one of the estate's cornfields—this is incredible history. Inclenberg was frequently spoken of as one of the loveliest spots on the island of Manhattan.

The section of New York City bounded by Midtown and Turtle Bay on the north, the East River on the east, Kips Bay and Rose Hill on the south, and what later became the garment center on the west became prominent. That area was called Murray Hill because that is where Mary and Robert Murray lived.

At the beginning of the Revolutionary War, many people remained undecided about their political preferences: Loyalists (British supporters) or Patriots (American supporters). Though her husband was a Loyalist (British supporter) and continued to buy British goods, Mary Lindley Murray was sympathetic to the American cause. Many family members were Revolutionaries and served in Washington's army, and she proved to be a true patriot despite her husband's loyalties to the British.

While her husband, Robert, tended to their farms and the acres of crops and livestock (which earned them much money), Mary worked independently. Mary was a very social person and a great hostess, providing crucial support to the colonial forces in the early days of the Revolutionary War.

In the days following the escape of the American forces after
the Battle of Long Island (August 1776), the first significant battle
between the Continentals and the British, General George Washington sent General Israel Putnam and 5,000 soldiers to New York
City. In mid-September, British warships took positions on Kip's
Bay to protect a flotilla of flat-bottomed boats that ferried 4,000
British soldiers to Manhattan.

On September 15, 1776, British troops led by General William
Howe landed in Kip's Bay, intending to attack and trap General
Putnam's troops, who were retreating in the face of far superior
numbers.

Mary Lindley Murray knew that Putnam's troops were within a
mile of her home and that these British forces were almost twice
the size of Putnam's army. Suppose Mary could stall the British
troops and warn Putnam's troops so that they could escape. She
came up with a plan.

Mary had a significant influence on her wealth in the community. She had more money than her neighbors, and it would be
noticed in the decorative facade of her home. After all, her home
was a place more talked about and desired in the area than any
other that she knew.

Mary knew she could invite the British to stay, and they would
see that as a friendly gesture with a loyalist. Little did the British
know that Mary had other plans since he tried to make her home a
friendly place for her visitors.

She regularly invited officers of the British forces stationed in
New York to her home. She wined and dined them, enabling them
to laugh and relax. She wanted them to believe that she favored the
British side during the revolution. She endeared herself and gained
their trust.

Again, during this one particular night, she had other ideas on
her mind. She wanted to ensure that there was plenty of food and

liquor so that these officers and their company would have plenty to talk about, eat, and drink. She helped take their minds off their responsibilities as members of the British army.

While they were doing this, which was Mary's idea in the first place, the Revolutionary forces of the colonies escaped from the trap set for them by the British army. When the British officers recovered from their drunkenness, they realized the Continental army had escaped; they set out to find them. Putman's forces dispersed east to Long Island, and some went north.

Mary succeeded in delaying them long enough for General Putnam to make an orderly retreat. In a journal entry on September 20, 1776, James Thatcher, a surgeon with the Continental army, recorded the incident, which is strong evidence of Mary's contribution to the American cause. David McCullough notes in his book *1776* that "she may have been extremely charming [to the British officers], but she was also a woman in her fifties and the mother of twelve children."

There is no definitive evidence concerning her true intentions on that September day. However, the legend of her actions speaks volumes of the effect women had on the Revolutionary War and how they could turn an everyday task like entertaining into an act of patriotism.

This is just one story that needs to be shared as part of our American history. It happened. It was significant. Mary Murray played an important role in history, yet we must search for these details because they are not a part of the history everyone knows. Women were discounted as having the ability to affect profound change in world affairs, so this story may be a surprise, but there were other women like her whose stories are unknown to most. America tries to tell all the stories of its history and not exclude the story of significance. It failed to remember this story, and it must be remembered.

Putnam was part of Washington's staff along with William Dawes and William Prescott. The British troops stopped Dawes and Prescott. However, Israel Putman was not stopped. Dawes and Prescott didn't ride along with Paul Revere. However, Revere might have gotten all the credit because of Henry Wadsworth Longfellow's famous poem - *The Midnight Ride of Paul Revere.* He didn't know about Dawes and Prescott.

The truth about this is that the only person who was able to complete his mission and warn the troops was Israel Putnam. Putnam was vitally important in getting the troops out physically. If Henry Wadsworth Longfellow had known about Mary Murray's influence on the Colonial army's escape, I wonder if the poem would have been written about her instead.

10

George Washington and John Adams

"It takes many good deeds to build a good reputation, and only one bad one to lose it."–Benjamin Franklin.

George Washington

George Washington is a name familiar to all of us. His role in American history was told to us, and his name was glorified in our history textbooks, but now it is time to share the truth.

Here are some quick facts to help bring you up to speed.

The First Continental Congress was held in the fall of 1774. The Second Continental Congress convened in Philadelphia in the summer of 1775, shortly after the war with the British had begun.

On July 4, 1776, Congress issued the Declaration of Independence, which asserted the colonies' intention to be entirely independent of England for the first time. The Congress established itself as the central governing authority under the Articles of Confederation, which remained in force until 1788.

Meanwhile, under the Articles of Confederation, the Second Continental Congress had decided to expand the nation and set their minds on acquiring territories around the Great Lakes. They were not wrong, but it might not have been appropriate then.

George Washington had another plan. According to what Thomas Jefferson had drafted and the Second Continental Congress eventually ratified, Washington was interested in paying off the country's debts from the Revolutionary War. He had borrowed money from Dutch Banks and other European banks to finance the recent war, and those banks were getting antsy. They wanted the new nation to start earnestly sending their promised payments.

However, Washington was not only going to pay off the debts, he was interested in another angle. He concocted a scheme whereby he would sell newly procured land within the parameters of the Northwest Ordinance.

Did you know that there were six actual Presidents for the American people and colonies before Washington was declared president of the United States of America? Let me introduce you to these men.

On March 2, 1781, Richard Henry Lee of Virginia served as the first President (of the Continental Congress) until the end of November 30, 1784. He was given an extension until November 4, 1785.

On March 22, 1788, after the convention, Cyrus Griffin was elected President of the Second Continental Congress. He served until March 2, 1789 (almost one year).

Peyton Randolph followed Griffin. After serving almost a year, he resigned due to bad health. Henry Middleton followed him, but Peyton Randolph, a very large strapping guy who liked his times at the tavern, was persuaded to return to the presidency. However, he was a blatant drunk. John Jay was then elected; following him was John Hancock, and finally Samuel Huntington.

These men were place keepers for the future presidency. They were the presidents of Continental Congresses. You might be shocked to know this, but this is the truth.

Congress appointed George Washington as the commander of the Continental Army and authorized the raising of the army through conscription.

For some background history, the First Continental Congress passed the Northwest Land Ordinance of 1785. They ratified it in 1787. Under the Articles of Confederation, land, and territories could be organized according to a certain amount of population and governors.

This ordinance indicated that purchased lands west of the Appalachian Mountains could be surveyed and sold. The region of the Northwest Territories included an area south of the Great Lakes, north and west of the Ohio River, and east of the Mississippi River.

The Northwest Territories also included the method of creating townships and sections within townships that were used to develop the United States' land after 1785.

A crucial part of the Northwest Ordinance was that it provided for civil liberties and public education but did not allow slavery. According to the National Archives, "a Bill of Rights protecting religious freedom, the right to a writ of habeas corpus, and the benefit of trial by the jury were among other rights that were discussed."

According to the historical account, editors in the Encyclopedia Britannica indicated that,

> The Northwest Territory must eventually comprise a minimum of three and a maximum of five states; an individual territory could be admitted to statehood in the Union after attaining a population of 60,000. Under the ordinance, slavery was forever outlawed from the lands of the Northwest Territory, freedom of religion and other civil liberties were guaranteed, the resident Indians were promised decent treatment, and education was provided for.

Washington decided to sell those lands for one dollar an acre to generate money to repay the Dutch, who had helped fund the revolution, and for personal gain. Things, however, were tumultuous. There was so much going on that the entire project had to be tabled.

By this time, new problems appeared. Issues were becoming more complex. The population was exploding. Nearly 700,000 inhabitants of our fledgling republic were enslaved, Black people. While this was happening, the vast majority, ninety percent, was concentrated in the Chesapeake area, and that population was growing exponentially.

No one was prepared to deal with this turn of events, and there were other distractions ahead. The situation regarding the large numbers of Native Americans still had to be considered, and very few were adequately prepared to begin to deal with that.

Following the American Revolutionary War and the Constitutional Convention, George Washington was elected President of the new United States on April 30th, 1789. This first public United States presidential election was held over several weeks, from

December 1788 to January 1789. Notice that the process of collecting votes was not limited to a single day; instead, it was held over several weeks. Washington was elected with every first-round ballot cast by the United States Electoral College. With this election, he became the only United States President to be unanimously chosen.

After his second unanimous election, his second term ended on March 8th, 1797. He had no opponent in either of his two elections. During his first term, several new states were admitted to our Union.

Those new states included North Carolina in 1788, Rhode Island in 1790, Vermont in 1791, Kentucky in 1792, and Tennessee in 1796. Washington's imprint on the early days of our nation was highlighted by his stance on non-involvement in foreign affairs, which is why he was not noted for his relationships with other countries.

Washington had little success in his first term. He simply tried to appease the northern and southern states, trying to be impartial. He offered no opinions, took no positions on issues, and stayed out of the fray. He did listen, but he rarely responded.

He had the formal authority granted by the Constitution as the country's first leader. He had selected a few good men for his first cabinet. He did have military experience, and those experiences gave him a chance to become a leader. Although he rarely offered an opinion and simply responded to each issue. (As a general, Washington's attention had strayed during the Revolutionary War, and Thomas Hickey, one member of his administrative staff, even tried to kill him because of this. Other officers stopped the attempt, and the General was removed from his position, and later, Hickey was court-martialed.)

Washington had other less violent exchanges, but he lost his concentration often and didn't follow up on problems, leaving others in his command to finish what he had started. He had a strong character, but his mind wandered to his property at Mount Vernon, his plantations, and his many slaves. He did not respect the Blacks on his plantation. He did not think those Blacks were equal to Whites.

Taking his personal life and lifestyle into account, he did not feel comfortable with the Constitution's recently ratified terms. The words in his oath, which he took when he was sworn in as President, were part of the Constitution. The meaning of these words never changed his behavior, and his opinions were never modified.

Martha Washington, who could read and write, was older than her husband. Martha was a widow with four children, only two of whom had survived to age five. Soon after her first husband died, she met and married George, who she remained with for a good part of the Revolutionary War. George and Martha had no children of their own. George might have been infertile because of his experiences earlier with tuberculosis and smallpox.

Martha brought her wealth to her second marriage and three hundred slaves. Because laws did not allow married women to own property, her seventeen thousand acres of land in several counties were put in George's name when she remarried. George liked owning her property, but he did not want to work the property, leaving that work to their slaves.

While he was president, George and Martha never lived in the White House. They lived in lower Manhattan, at the President's home designated by the convention.

Following the Constitutional Convention, the first American Congress convened. This Congress was preoccupied with completing the product that the recently ended Convention produced, which was our Constitution. However, the convention had a skeleton outline, and the first Congress was convened to expand on it.

Twenty-nine representatives attended these meetings, and their job was, according to Article one of the Constitution, to create and finance the government departments and produce a revenue stream. According to Articles One and Two, they had to deal with staffing the government and providing oaths to obtain their loyalty to get these departments functioning. It was also consumed with establishing a government that could deal with its other proscribed constitutional duties.

At the same time, the new president was attempting to set up his office with the help of the secretary the staff had provided. What his secretary did is unknown because the office was not established. The President had his horse, and it was reported that he was riding around to visit people. These visits were not more than a ceremonial function. However, his popularity rose as citizens had a chance to observe their president. He was becoming a citizen of renown, but he remained aloof. Few, if any, of the attendees at the Convention even knew him. Most of them had not voted for him, but now he was out with his horse, meeting people, trying to seem amiable, and meeting those who had *no opportunity to vote for him* because that was done in the Convention, behind closed doors. But, there he was, their president, presenting himself for all to see. He did not engage on *any* level, but there he was. He was their President, even if they had no opportunity to vote for him or speak to him.

No one was prepared to deal with anything substantive, and many other distractions were ahead. The situation regarding the dozens of Native Americans still had to be considered. There were very few who were adequately prepared to deal with that.

However, from the plan that lay before them, they tabled the discussion that had to take place; that was the issue of slavery. But it was so much more than that. So much had to be done to create the actual government, but there was no basis from which to begin the work, and those in power were not thinking about the nation as a whole; they were only thinking about themselves.

Slavery involved the concepts of freedom, equality, and tolerance; those discussions were delayed as if they would settle themselves. Lincoln later said, "a house divided against itself cannot stand." If those words had been uttered in the eighteenth century, no one would have paid attention to them, nor would anyone have remembered them. Some historians have labeled the late 18th century as the Age of Passion. But for whom and what were they passionate? They certainly weren't paying attention to or expressing and passion for their country because they were not involved.

Washington may have been virtuous and subordinated some of his interests on behalf of the people, but he was mentally detached during his presidency. He did not give great speeches or share his opinions, but with his stature and reputation, he was respected. The point of George Washington was that he was the face of freedom and as well as being the face of America.

Washington did not retain his mental capacity; he was almost senile. At this point, he could argue that the federal government's authority would have to be expanded to compensate for his lack of presence. Years before, an editor had labeled Washington a traitor because they thought he had conspired with the English government during the War.

Later, it came to light that the charges were based on forged English documents. It was a strange time in the closing days of the eighteenth century.

Washington had set a precedent that lasted for a long time – that a President should only serve two terms. After leaving the presidency, he returned to his plantation to continue to attend to his land, whiskey distillery business, and pigs. He opposed the imposition of taxes on his whiskey operation, even though those taxes were only around $300 a year. He assumed a role in the Whiskey Rebellion in 1794 to oppose those taxes. Washington made large sums of money from his whiskey operation, making him one of the wealthiest entrepreneurs in American history.

Washington was enamored with the life of a country gentleman. Even though that lifestyle was predicated on the abundance of Martha's money and the perpetuation of slavery as an "American Institution."

As he died, Washington was seen taking his pulse.

Washington's death gave way so that John Adams could now occupy center stage; that was especially the case here. Our third election would involve more people and feature two candidates.

But, the election of 1796 had the potential to be more democratic! Perhaps it would present a chance for more people of America to participate and have their voices heard. That would be a change! But would that mean that this change would make a difference—America wasn't ready for that kind of change.

However, after George died, Martha set the enslaved people free.

Since England put the slavery issue to rest by abolishing it, they had little concern for slavery going forward.

John Adams (1735-1826)

John Adams became our second president and was known as a very outspoken advocate for independence in the Second Continental Congress. John Adams was a well-known political official but was not so highly regarded as a politician even though he had a law degree. Some observed that he was obnoxious, unpopular, and full of hubris, which matched his ambition.

His colleagues viewed Adams as "impetuous, vain, and highly opinionated." It was almost tribal. Adams was supposed to be a statesman. He was not a governor or a military commander. The party of the Federalists was incompatible with Adams's thoughts. Adams thought he was supposed to transcend like a Patriot King. Adams didn't take to this. He was supposed to manage this, but he didn't do that. Adams rarely talked to his cabinet, and it was no secret that Adams and Jefferson despised each other and did not take counsel from one another. Nevertheless, somehow out of tradition and respect for the office and out of integrity and intellect, Adams commanded respect as the President.

He had been our first Vice President, and then he became our second President. Adams failed to maintain the regard he commanded as Washington's Vice President but managed to finish one term.

One can hardly mention John Adams without mentioning Abigail Adams. As a child, Abigail was sickly, and since she had been home for a long time, she had full access to her father's library. She became well-read and educated, formed opinions, and kept to them. She was remembered as one being "sharp, shrewd, insightful, but somewhat puritanical and even, on occasion, judgmental."

Abigail had a strong sense of right and wrong. She had little to no patience with men's views of females as the weaker sex. She stood her ground and needed to as she was married to John Adams. We remember her letter to John Adams on March 31, 1776, when she wrote: "Remember the Ladies."

> *I long to hear that you have declared an independency. And, by the way, in the new code of laws which I suppose it will be necessary for you to make, I desire you would remember the ladies and be more generous and favorable to them than your ancestors. Do not put such unlimited power into the hands of the husbands. Remember, all men would be tyrants if they could. If particular care and attention is not paid to the ladies, we are determined to foment a rebellion and will not hold ourselves bound by any laws in which we have no voice or representation.*

These words were heard in the 18th century but didn't manifest until the late 19th century.

This letter, and the hundreds she wrote to friends and family over her lifetime, revealed her strength of character, opinions, and love for John. Remember that Adams was hot-headed, and his wife, Abigail, was composed and intelligent and true beauty. John would not have made it as far as he did without Abigail.

Now John faced two significant problems in his presidency; the first was a diplomatic one which resulted in an undeclared war provoked partly by the XYZ affair. The more severe event that followed soon after that was that of Adams' Alien and Sedition Acts.

According to the National Library of Study for George Washington, "The XYZ Affair was a moment within this larger span of events tying the domestic and international arenas together as the Federalists benefited politically from a French attempt to bribe American diplomats. Yet the Federalist reaction to the XYZ affair would eventually cause a backlash against them and contribute substantially to the election of Thomas Jefferson to the presidency in 1800."

According to some historians, John Adams was confronted with the dilemma of a possible global war between the French and the English. There was also a conflict between the Federalists and their opponents. The basis of that discussion was whether the new republic should side with the English or the French or remain as neutral as possible.

Jefferson and Madison did not want war with France. Adams had an alliance with England in his mind, but Jefferson had friendships with the French.

From 1783-1812, the United States was in a precarious position. The government was unstable, and the promises made by the Continental Congress remained unfulfilled. The new government and the military were unable to contend with foreign enemies and domestic unrest and what the new United States needed most was stability at home and legitimacy abroad.

Adams was the real cause of the War of 1812. Jefferson and Madison thought that Adams had concocted the XYZ affair as a declaration of war and included bribery to make it happen.

Following this, John Adams had to face the Alien and Sedition Acts. These four laws placed restrictions on aliens living in the United States and made it harder to maintain the concept of freedom of speech. At that time, thinking for oneself was not prized or even appreciated!

According to history, "A series of laws known collectively as the Alien and Sedition Acts was passed by the Federalist Congress in 1798 and signed into law by President Adams. These laws included new powers to deport foreigners and make it harder for new immigrants to vote. Previously a new immigrant would have to reside in the United States for five years before becoming eligible to vote, but a new law raised the requirement to 14 years."

According to the Alien and Sedition Acts conceived by Abigail Adams, making false or defamatory statements about the national government or President Adams became illegal. Freedom of speech had been protected by the Constitution before then.

In today's world, the Alien and Sedition Acts would be considered unconstitutional since they decried the parts of the new Constitution that limited free speech. Jefferson and Madison challenged these actions maintaining the position that the Alien and Sedition Acts betrayed the ideals of the new Constitution by exceeding the limited powers that were given to the national government by the Constitution.

Citizens believed that this extension of power was an encroachment that went beyond the limits of the law. If states could disregard federal law, the federal government believed it could not enforce it everywhere. That would become a festering problem, and it would only get worse.

In October of 1797, Alexander Hamilton published a pamphlet calling President Adams' decisions as president "irrational and identifying Adams as impulsive and unfit to be president."

The political parties were well on their way to settling the country into a two-party system. John Adams was on the traditional side that restricted participation in our democracy, and Jefferson, on the other side, preferred a more open democracy, but the problems with American politics had been born. The fight to have, or not have, enslaved people was at the heart of that problem. The conflict would eventually lead to civil war nearly sixty years later.

Of course, that war was not civil. It created hate and fear, resulting in conflict between all new arrivals in America and the political forces engaged in power politics that were already here. It

even tore apart the friendship of Adams and Jefferson. They were
not able to communicate with one another for nearly twenty years.

Do you see the impact politics can have on a nation being torn
apart and within some friendships? The relationship between John
Adams and Thomas Jefferson, though their relationship was
partially restored via letters before their deaths, it was never again
to be what it once was.

In the election of 1796, John Adams ran, and his vote totals
showed that he had defeated Thomas Jefferson. Jefferson, though,
would become our second vice president.

As Jefferson became the president, Adams set the tone for how
the power would be transferred to the next president—with peace.
Adams left early in the morning of Jefferson's inauguration to meet
with his family and allow the next president the opportunity to
move into his new residence.

11

Jefferson and Madison

**"Knowledge will bring you
the opportunity to make a difference." – Claire Fagin**

Thomas Jefferson

Jefferson was born on April 14, 1743, and died on July 4th,
1826, the same day that John Adams passed. The day he died had
been fifty years since the day that the Declaration of Independence
was signed.

He is best remembered for writing our Declaration of Independence in 1776 and his election to the presidency in 1800, when he
became our third president.

He liked to read, was an architect, loved sculpture, and is
credited with founding the University of Virginia. He was
extremely curious about many things like prehistory, paleontology,
and woolly mammoths. He also wrote the Virginia Statute for
religious freedom.

As a delegate to the Second Continental Congress, he wrote laws that would prohibit slavery in America, and these writings were then incorporated into the Thirteenth Amendment after the Civil War. However, isn't it ironic that long before the war, Jefferson wrote the words of freedom and equality, but his lifestyle never applied to those words? Talk about calling the kettle Black!

Slavery existed everywhere, from America to Africa and in the Caribbean. In the 15th century, Portuguese traders stole enslaved Black people from trading vessels and sold them in Europe for profit. A large percentage of the enslaved people came from the West African country of Niger. Many of those enslaved people became residents of the island of Jamaica.

Ninety percent of the businesses of slave traders obtained enslaved people in the Atlantic region and brought those enslaved people to America. This was an extremely profitable business.

Jefferson owned many enslaved people. When Thomas Jefferson and Martha Wayles wed, Thomas Jefferson's father and Martha Wayles's father (John Wayles) gave them at least several hundred enslaved Black people as a wedding gift.

According to deeper research, John Wayles had a first wife (Martha Epps). Martha Epps gave birth to Martha Wayles. Now, on the other side of the coin, John Wayles also had at least one slave concubine named Elizabeth Hemings. Elizabeth bore six children with John Wayles. One of those children was called Sally Hemings. So technically, Martha Wayles (25 years older) and Sally Hemings (25 years younger) were half-sisters. Upon John Wayles's death, Elizabeth Hemings and her children (including Sally) were given to Thomas Jefferson and Martha.

The business of *slavery* is a black mark upon the founding of America and the Founding Fathers—especially upon the life of Thomas Jefferson. Unfortunately, the black mark was not extended to them until the 21st century—when the truth is finally being discussed.

Until then, during his life before becoming president, during Jefferson's presidency, and after his two terms, Jefferson bought and sold slaves, and no one thought otherwise! That's just the way it was. Later in his administration, Jefferson purchased a second plantation further south along the Mississippi River. He brought more enslaved people to perform the work required on that plantation. Jefferson hired men to keep those slaves in line. He continued his business on those plantations while he was our third president. Jefferson owned at least four hundred slaves at his plantation in Monticello in the state of Virginia at Charlottesville.

After the prohibition of the slave trade in 1809, Jefferson resorted to finding another way to increase his slave property and wealth. He decided to have children with one of his slaves. He chose Sally Hemings.

According to research, Sally traveled with Jefferson to places outside of the union, like Europe. Sally was fourteen years old. She was selected to be the maidservant to Thomas and Martha Jefferson's daughter, Maria. Sally Hemings performed her duties as a maidservant and was technically *free* while in France.

After nearly eighteen months in France, Sally became pregnant with Thomas Jefferson's child. Sally was now sixteen. Jefferson was never embarrassed by his behavior. He believed those Black human beings were his property, and sex, slavery, and being the master was part of his entitlement as an enslaver!

Before returning to America, Sally negotiated with one of the nation's most powerful men to improve her condition. Sally would only return to America if Jefferson extended "extraordinary privileges" to her. Sally wanted *free♦om for her future chil♦ren.* According to the record given by one of her sons, Madison, Thomas Jefferson agreed. Madison recalled, "Sally *implicitly relie♦* on Jefferson's promise." Hemings also said that he and his siblings "were the only children of [Jefferson's] by a slave woman."

After returning to Virginia, Sally delivered the child, and it lived but a short time. No other record of that child has been found.

Jefferson and Sally Hemings had several more children together—a total of six. However, only four would live to adulthood. Through the *extraor♦inary privileges,* Sally won the freedom of all four children: two of her children walked to freedom in 1822, and her two other children were freed upon Thomas Jefferson's death in 1826.

Sally herself was never legally emancipated. Instead, she was unofficially freed—or "given her time"—by Jefferson's daughter Martha after his death.

Jefferson professed to love liberty, but he owned human beings as enslaved people! Again, his written word would move us toward integration, but by his actions, he didn't believe that Black people were equal to White people.

When will people learn that our actions speak louder than our words?

Throughout his life, he called slavery "a moral depravity." Publicly, he opposed slavery and said that he thought that slavery would come to be called "the greatest threat to America's survival."

History portrays Thomas Jefferson with uncommon adjectives for his thoughts and his two terms as president at the start of the 19th century. Jefferson was brilliant in many roles. He is remembered for his words, his thoughts, and his writings. But he was, as many historians have said, not without glaring holes in his thought processes, and he should be remembered for his misdeeds. Jefferson was brilliant. He could put words together and explain what he wanted to explain, but the behavior he exhibited behind those words and how he lived his life was simply another thing.

These facts were evident, and if people took the time to read Jefferson's written words in our history books, it would be an affront to our democracy.

After recognizing Jefferson's real truth and flaws as a man, we must look at what Thomas Jefferson contributed to America as a statesman. Jefferson thought the government was an instrument created purposefully for their protection, allowing the people as much freedom to pursue their goals and ambitions as possible.

Jefferson thought that the right to citizenship in America must be expanded. He sought changes for the families of these White citizens and their offspring.

Now, there is an incredible contribution that Jefferson made to the United States. One of these mighty changes was The Louisiana Purchase. It was a seminal moment for a new nation. The Louisiana Purchase was over 830,000 square miles and eventually would encompass 15 states.

In 1800, the vast region was basically under French control after Napoleon reached an agreement with Spain. As we have read earlier, Jefferson was very familiar with the French and understood France's potential military danger if they controlled the Mississippi River. That was just too close to the American border for Jefferson's liking.

Jefferson sent James Monroe to France in 1803 to negotiate the deal. Jefferson said to Monroe, "all eyes, all hopes, are now fixed on you, . . . for on the event of this mission depends the future destinies of this republic."

After several weeks of negotiations, Monroe made a deal for the $15 million purchase on July 4, 1803. The Louisiana Purchase, through the eyes of Jefferson, was done through a Constitutional amendment. However, Jefferson's cabinet, including James Madison, disagreed about the need for a Constitutional amendment. It was permissible and implied under the Consitution's treaty-making provisions, so the purchase was made. The Senate, by treaty, ratified the purchase in October of 1803.

Other accomplishments by Jefferson as President were:

1. He slashed Army and Navy expenditures,
2. He cut the budget,
3. He eliminated the tax on whiskey
4. He reduced the national debt by a third.

These accomplishments are great and helpful for the country, but my mind is continually drawn back to a few things about Jefferson.

To re-emphasize, Jefferson wrote pretty words for our Declaration of Independence, but he did not believe those words!

What did the concepts mean *to form a more perfect union*?
What did the words *all men are created equal* mean to him?
What did *inalienable rights* mean to him?
What did *liberty* mean to him?
In fact, what did *justice for all* mean to him?

He had no value for the concept of equality. He wrote those words and endorsed them! However, he did not practice what he preached or wrote. These words remained only words. Two centuries later, those ideals still had not been fully realized.

The words of Jefferson might inspire those of us in America, but we have never approached the possibility that those ideals could become a permanent part of the American fabric.

Our country needs to start dealing with what it is, then make choices to find paths that will help us improve things. We can change a jungle into a thriving beacon on a hill but let's always remember that we started as a jungle.

Remember that seventeen of the 55 delegates at the Philadelphia Convention in 1787 owned more than 1,400 slaves! Let us also remember that these seventeen men and many others were considered to be among our first heroes.

Let's stop for a moment to consider Jefferson an educated man. He believed that the people were the surest safeguards of Liberty and that the remedy for their mistakes was to inform their discretion with education. Jefferson believed that laws and institutions had to change along with the development of the human mind, and he expressed that by making plans for the University of Virginia. He read a great many books and had a great library which he later sold to the Library of Congress.

Before becoming president, Jefferson had an idea for founding a great university. His re-invention was begun when he founded the University of Virginia in Charlottesville. The plan was to find a new method to advance human knowledge, educate leaders, and attempt to cultivate an informed body that would advance learning.

The plan was to create a working relationship between the students and the faculty so that they could live and learn from each

other. This *academic village* was a sizeable spread-out area with vast
expansive buildings, lawns, and trees that provided shade and space
surrounded by Jefferson's favorite art forms derived from classical
architecture.

Many of the builders of this campus were enslaved Blacks who
had been convicted of crimes, and while serving their sentences,
they were constructing the campus without *pay*. As they
constructed the buildings, they did so under the sharp eye of a
master. Isn't it ironic that the structures of truth and knowledge
were built at the hands of enslaved people? They were kept from
the education they helped to build. For centuries, Blacks were not
admitted to learning there. Note: The first African American
gained admission to the University of Virginia, as a student, on
September 15, 1950.

Most of the seventy professors owned enslaved people who had
duties to perform from early morning to late at night. They were
now obligated to perform their morning work, walk to the university, help clean, and prepare the work for the professors.
Following that, they had to return by walking back to their village
to complete the day's work. This burden added three to six miles of
extra walking throughout the day.

With this model of using this cheap source of labor set by the
University of Virginia, other universities like Yale and Harvard,
and many others took advantage of the Blacks while engaging in
the slave trade and the substantial hiring of these Blacks. All of this
was through private efforts, restricting the attainment of racial
equality while hiding the truth.

Most faculty claimed that "veritas," meaning truth, is our motto,
but it is more than that. It is our reason for being. We are committed to the truth for the sake of our community or nation. But did
those professors practice it? What were they teaching? *Do as I say,*

not as I do. There was a disconnect—an academic gap—from applying the knowledge of hope and freedom (because they all were
enslavers).

Jefferson's attempt to create a place of safety and learning seems
to have another ironic stain that history swept under the rug. The
very places of education, debate, and truth were built with the
knowledge that the same hands who erected the structures would
never see the truth given to them in their lifetime. That would
have to come later—much later.

Something to note here was that Jefferson also believed in a
living Constitution. He conceived the philosophy that our Constitution should be revised at stated intervals. These periods should
be planned ahead of time. After all, every twenty years or so, a new
majority will attain political power, the right to vote, and seek to
become independent of previous generations who formed a
majority in their time.

It was a new era when these younger people came of age and
wanted to replace thoughts that were part of what the previous
generation had used to create their majority. They believed this
new generation now had a right to choose their path and promote
changes as a new generation aspired to establish.

Jefferson had the moral authority, even though he would
discuss, develop and maintain concessions and seek consensus
independent of other groups. This idea would seek to establish a
new relevance for each succeeding generation.

So, dear reader, how would you grade this country—based on
her words or actions?

People follow others reverently without pursuing their paths.
Aristotle philosophized that each citizen is responsible for the

types of moral character he develops. He called it "creating and developing each man's moral courage" to think about what he wanted and find his path in life. Few thinkers in that millennia had been lauded for their moral courage. The same thing persists today in the 21st century, but who is accredited with having moral courage today?

One of the significant controversies of the Philadelphia Convention was over the basis of citizenship, or as we would call it now, voting qualifications. We need to examine what the cause of that citizenship should be. When people were born in other countries and came to America, along with many others who came here before them, there was a place known by that name—*America*.

Why did Jefferson and other Founders allow skin color to be a considering factor of who is *property* and who is not? Why only skin color? *Why* wasn't height a consideration or weight? *Why* not the color of each person's tongue? *Why* can't people be considered equals? *Why* do people have to be asked so many questions by people with little interest in knowing the answers to those questions?

Why can't we believe that people who do not look like us have a right to be near and live alongside us? *Why* don't we consider that each of us has something that makes us different and distinct from everyone else? *Why* don't we find commonality and enjoy each other despite the differences we see?

In the third century BC, Aristotle wrote that "the state is to be ruled for its citizens' benefit." This state must promote the issues and virtues of each citizen. Therefore, all the members of the society should possess the power to elect officials and hold them accountable. This country must not exclude any large body of people from participation and power. If it does, it creates enemies of the state.

Collectively these masses possess judgment, and their reasoning is valid, so these states should listen. Aristotle stated that "the best state is based on the middle class because it arrives at the best possible compromise." Usually, that compromise is the only one capable of maintaining a stable government. Why should it be that way?

Based on that, we had the great compromise of the Constitution to shout freedom and yet continue with slavery. Jefferson was very good at it. Jefferson lorded over everybody, but that was the tradition. In that era, it was just the way it was.

There's still time to get this right.

There is a *Second Chance* for everyone who lives today; to learn from Jefferson all his mistakes, not repeat them, and make the future better for everyone.

James Madison

James Madison wrote the Bill of Rights, comprised of the first ten amendments of the U.S. Constitution, which was introduced on June 8th, 1789. He is known as the "Father of our Constitution." When he wrote those amendments, he said "no state shall violate the equal rights of conscience," yet he condoned slavery. From the very start, the application of the Bill of Rights has been a falsehood.

Madison believed that all governmental power originates with the people. He declared that the people possessed an inalienable right to reform their government whenever they felt it was inadequate. These powers were instituted to guarantee the rights of the people to acquire property. Under those rights, people should be able to maintain safety and provide for their happiness.

Throughout Madison's writings, he proclaimed that *all* humans were entitled to be recognized as equals and should be free. He said that all of us possessed a natural right to our own religious beliefs in addition to the right to freedom and the right to have a free conscience.

However, he did not believe that when it came to his life. He owned hundreds of enslaved Black people but gave them no consideration or thought. America was seen as a land of equality that advanced the concept of toleration, but Madison did not understand the concept of equality. The idea of equality had no application in practice to him.

America was expected to be open to the oppressed in the world. Instead, we are available to crime, prejudice, hate, and bigotry. We are intolerant of many other beliefs. However, we are entitled to a *Secon‹ Chance*—we can still change.

The Federalist papers were written to convince the state of New York to join a movement to keep the thirteen colonies together and produce what became our Constitution. In Federalist No. X, Madison tried to give a realistic view of the promises of the Constitution and provided rules that would contain and prevent flaws that would lead to division in America, but Madison misunderstood the logic and the nature of dealing with a limited amount of individual freedom.

Freedom allows each person the right to have their thoughts. These thoughts do not destroy liberty, which is essential to the existence of all of us. However, it gives every citizen the right to express their opinions, passions, and interests equally. Madison continued when he said, "Liberty is to faction, like "air is to fire, an ailment without which it instantly expires." However, it could not be less folly to abolish liberty, which is essential to political life.

Madison believed that as long as there is a connection between man's ability to reason and speak his opinions and feel his passion, all men could have a reciprocal influence on each other. The diversity in these opinions is not an insurmountable obstacle to the expression of interests; in fact, the protection of this expression is the first object of government. But was this practical?

The voicing of opinions concerning government can divide humanity into political forces where they can work toward agreement and perhaps provide a path that can lead to change. But other roads go in different directions, and that choice is up to you when you reach the crossroads.

Madison said, "justice should hold the balance between all of these different parties that express thought and that these thoughts create forces that strive to prevail."

He went on to say that regulating these various interfering interests forms the principal task of modern legislation. But, he added that justice ought to hold the balance between these competing thoughts and their eventual acceptance.

Alexis de Tocqueville wrote a book called *The Real Advantages That America Derives From Democratic Government.* He pointed out that "laws of American democracy are frequently defective or incomplete." He pointed out that a "distinction must be carefully observed between the end to which these forces aim and how they are directed."

de Tocqueville said, "the purpose of a democracy and the conduct of its legislation should be useful to the greatest number of citizens." But he also said, however, that "this was the total of the advantages of democracy." In a democracy, the laws are almost always ineffective; but there exists in the concept of democracy the possibility of making these laws more perfect. However, de Tocqueville never addressed the question, "Why is this the case?"

Thus, we can provide the means so that more people can participate. This leads us to the fact that if we create a majority so that the people can decide, we have done our job. Therefore if we provide choices, we have achieved our goal and contributed to the well-being of the most significant number of people. But is that always the case?

The men entrusted with discussing public affairs in the United States are frequently inferior in capacity and morality. Corruption may affect the role of the government. The goal is to create and ensure the greatest happiness for the most significant number of citizens.

de Tocqueville points out that all community members should immediately be granted political rights. But, he neglects the next part; the question is, *to whom* should these political rights be granted? Should these rights be given to *all people*, or should only some possess these rights? *Everybo•y* should possess these rights.

de Tocqueville said that there are no great nations and that there would never be a great society without the notion of individual rights. People in each community must be allowed the peaceful exercise of certain rights; this is inalienable. Democracy brings the idea of political rights to every citizen. This is one of the most significant advantages of democracy.

There is a fantastic strength in the expression of the determination of a majority. When ideas were written throughout the United States, except for enslaved people, servants, and paupers, all other classes of persons directly contributed to making our laws. Those who plan and carry out attacks against those laws must either modify the opinion of the nation or else just trample on its decision. Everyone in America should be personally interested in enforcing the obedience of the whole community to the law.

The framers of the Constitution were also careful to arrange matters so that a majority could win control over only a part of the government at one time. Madison thought, as did most of the framers of the Constitution, that the legislative branch was the most likely to take over the whole government.

"In republican government," Madison wrote, "the legislative authority necessarily predominates." That was because, he thought, that divided the legislature in two and made each branch responsible to different constituencies. One of the branches would be more accountable to the changing whims and opinions, and they would be up for election every two years.

The members of the other branch of Congress would serve for a longer term, and only one-third of that body would be up for election every two years.

"Independent judges" were necessary, said Alexander Hamilton in Federalist No. 78, because he felt those judges would be an essential safeguard against the changing opinions of society. But Why? It looks like we need to reexamine this in the 21st century.

Madison wrote in The Federalist that "the great difficulty lies in this: we must first enable the government to direct the governed, and we must also enable the government to control itself."

Therefore, any new Constitution would become more than just a symbol. It needed to present a plan. It should be an instrument granting and limiting the power of the government, without extinguishing people's rights.

In this way, the Constitution is both a positive instrument allowing the government to control the governed and a restraint on government by which the governed can check those in power.

This is the system of federalism.

Edmund Burke (1729 to 1797), a British-born writer, wrote that "the only thing necessary for evil to succeed is for good men (and women) to do nothing." Freedom of the Press and Freedom of Speech does not protect sedition. That's where we are.

Detracting from what Americans were trying to achieve created seditionists because people were not educated, factions grew and created distance between people. Our Declaration and our Constitution did not necessarily protect their words. Their words crossed the line and were not protected. The precepts did not preserve their violence in any of our documents. Our valued ideals were precepts and didn't stand the test of practice. These words are their opinions, but they were not part of the concept of free speech.

We should not be permitted to shout "fire" in a crowded theater or stand up in an organized meeting and distract everyone by shouting vile words and making physical gestures.

12

Adding More Powder to the Keg

"The most common way
people give
up their power is by thinking
they don't have any."
-Alice Walker.

During the days of Jefferson, another man deserves to be mentioned. His name was William Ellery Channing. Channing was born in Newport, Rhode Island, and graduated from Harvard in 1798. Then, for the following two years, he worked as a tutor in Richmond, Virginia, and spent considerable time in private study.

During this period, Channing underwent a profound religious experience, and in 1801 he returned to Harvard for theological study. He was ordained the minister of Boston's Federal Street Congregational Church in 1803 and held this pastorate throughout his life.

Channing believed in Unitarianism. Unitarianism rejects the mainstream Christian doctrine of the Trinity, or three persons in one God, made up of Father, Son, and the Holy Spirit. They typically believe that God is one being, hence the word Unitarianism.

Channing was a Unitarian minister and a transcendentalist. He was also a friend of Ralph Waldo Emerson. Channing had a benevolent view of God and was part of the eighteenth-century Enlightenment. The path to transcendentalism found its way through Unitarianism.

Ralph Waldo Emerson described Channing as "one of those men who vindicate the power of the *American race* to produce greatness."

Channing's life influenced the New England Transcendentalists. Like Jean-Jacques Rousseau, whose writings he admired, he was partly an Enlightenment figure and a romantic. Together, they produced a concept of what it means to be a good person. Channing admired Jean-Jacques Rousseau, who stated that "man in nature is guided by instinct only, whereas, in society, morality and justice are goals side by side."

Channing's romanticism is most apparent in the sermon "Likeness to God" (1828), in which he asserted that humankind discovers God through scripture and rational inquiry and consciousness. Long before Emerson's famous essays were published, Channing was preaching that in all its higher actions, the soul had "a character of infinity" and described sin as "the ruin of God's noblest work."

Although Channing never professed enthusiasm for the *new views*, the similarity between his conception of the divine potential in human nature and the later pronouncements of Emerson is unmistakable.

As we can see from Channing's philosophical and theological thinking, the value of humanity is a huge priority. Channing had written about slavery, abolition, and emancipation. The challenge was that the conflict between free and enslaved states must stop. He provided ethical support to the cause of abolition and the moral issue of human rights. Still, he disagreed with many of the points made in the discussions on slavery he witnessed.

In one of the most lucid statements of American leaders on behalf of free speech, free press, and free discussion, Channing took the side of the abolitionists. The abolitionists were crusaders for the enslaved Black people, but they carried with them the most sacred rights of being human. They were never all free men and believed that Black and White men were equal. (Notice there was no mention of women.) The following words were published in 1848. Jefferson had passed away and was not there to hear Channing's words.

> "The defenders of freedom are not those who claim and exercise rights which no one assails, for who win shouts of applause by well-turned compliments to liberty in the days of her triumph. They are those who stand up for the rights, which mobs, conspiracies, or single tyrants put in jeopardy, who contend for Liberty in that particular form which is threatened at the moment by the many or the few."

Perhaps, Jefferson should have still been alive to hear Channing speak, so he could have rethought and finally understood and internalized the words he had written years before to finally understand what they actually meant.

In his essay on slavery, Channing drew up a philosophical basis for emancipating enslaved people. If an enslaved person was property, when did that enslaved person cease being a human being? If an enslaved person was not property, how could that person be owned? The moral contention that no man could be claimed as property by another thus had to be a self-evident truth! Thomas Jefferson never considered that.

Taking this one step further, Channing believed that no man could be held as property because he has human rights, and, by extension, so does *every* person who exists! All humans possess these same rights! This was the fundamental morality attributed to every person.

To subject a man to slavery was to deny him all the rights he was entitled to as a human being; he also retained the power to assert those rights. Finally, no man could be claimed as property by another person, and this moral contention was, therefore, a self-evident truth. Does the duration of a wrong ever make it right?

I think the truth is to be found in the words of our forefathers. The rights and freedoms of our Constitution say that all men are created equal. I am positive that it does. Thomas Jefferson was not there to hear those words being uttered. Perhaps every formerly enslaved person was entitled to a "redress of grievances." I am sure that if positions were reversed, White men and women would have been in court long ago.

Now, I must share my insights about Andrew Jackson. It started in the third decade of the 19th century—1830. Andrew Jackson had just won the Presidency, and with it, he felt he had ultimate power. We all know that power doth corrupt, which is what happened with Jackson.

Jackson's inaugural speech was not long—only ten minutes. He promised to end the national debt and keep the size of the federal government small. He made his stand against corruption and reform. After the address, the crowd cheered wildly.

That was the only time they cheered for him. You see, Jackson worked behind the scenes to get his friends and allies appointed to the proper Congressional committees to produce a bill congruent with his desires—the Indian Removal Act.

The new law now fully committed the United States government to a policy of Native American removal, a policy that Jackson and his allies would bring to life in the latter years of his presidency.

Why did Jackson want to remove the native people? He declared that removal would "incalculably strengthen the southwestern frontier." But, who would this benefit? Not the Native Americans. When Jackson spoke to Congress, he proclaimed that clearing Alabama and Mississippi of their Native American populations would "enable those states to advance rapidly in population, wealth, and power."

His message contained many observations, assessments, and prejudices about Native Americans that American policymakers had widely held since Thomas Jefferson's presidency. According to Jackson, White settlements in the east were expanding, the range for Native American hunters was diminishing, and so was the land available for settlers from the east who wanted to move west.

According to historians, Jackson persuasively argued that this expansion would gradually lead to the extinction of the Native Americans. Jackson's theme was repeated repeatedly; Native Americans needed to be resettled on vacant lands west of the Mississippi River for their good and survival.

Upon hearing that, Congress passed the Indian Removal Act. It forcibly sanctioned the relocation of the Creek, Chickasaw, Cherokee, Choctaw, and Seminole tribes to land allotments west of the Mississippi River. Congress then passed the ninety-four removal treaties following the bill's enactment. From 1835 to 1838, the Cherokee and Creek nations were forcibly removed from the Southeast onto reservations west of the Mississippi. Nearly one-quarter of them died during the process of what became known as the "Trail of Tears."

How could this tragedy happen on the soil of America? It is simple—two words: wealth and power. But you must ask yourself, wealth and power for whom? Andrew Jackson was considered a tyrant because he removed the Native Americans, overused veto-ing, and the general fact that he just "showed more contempt!"

Andrew Jackson would not allow any bills to pass and used the veto power as a King would hold a scepter. Jackson rejected decisions or proposals made by Congress again and again. The overall reason Jackson is known to be a tyrant is his abuse of power.

The Indian Removal Act was a move against a nation's people that forced Native Americans into weakened positions from which they never recovered.

Andrew Jackson was the epitome of a tyrant. People were given no voice, no rights, and no power to fight off his actions. They were forced into a march that left more blood on the fabric of America. In one act by the government, the Native Americans who were here first, who had established nations in America long before the Constitution was ever written, lay defeated and emo-tionally slaughtered. Although there weren't enslaved people, freedom and equality were *not* extended to them. Again, more blood spilled in the land we call America.

Those who witnessed this act seemed to add more powder to the keg that was heating up and getting ready to burst. Americans were becoming increasingly aware because of the newspaper; the ability to read and write became more frequent for the average American.

Next, I must provide some history from Frederick Law Olmstead (1822-1903). Olmstead was an early artist but possessed many other talents. Olmstead wrote a book in 1861. It was called *The Cotton King•om*. His premise in that book was to attempt to determine whether slavery was good or bad.

Frederick Olmstead began his project intending to try to remain impartial. He tried to ascertain whether slavery was worthwhile. Statistics alone showed that every enslaved Black person costs the owner of that enslaved person $120.00 per year just to feed and provide shelter in Virginia.

In New York, the cost of shelter was less. There it was $108.00 to feed and house each Black laborer. Allowing for the fact that enslavers must provide clothing for their slaves and free laborers were better fed, it was 25% more expensive in the rural South for slave owners.

The poor Whites in the South considered it degrading to perform work that a Black person might otherwise perform. Was that equality?

Olmstead points out that areas with more Black inhabitants were more shoddy and rundown, more in need of repair and upkeep. Poor Whites would simply ignore what needed to be done if they were in the vicinity of Blacks.

Besides, these Whites did not want to be seen doing what Blacks were supposed to do. Access to education and acceptance of equality was not part of this equation. The poor Whites lost hope and did not pursue education or upward mobility because they felt it was hopeless. Blacks would not be educated because the law restricted—the ability to get an education; the pursuit of upward mobility needed to be open to all.

What slavery eventually proved to Olmstead was that slavery was not economically beneficial, except it enabled the enslavers to not have to perform specific tasks themselves. Slavery also was there to indicate the moral clarity to the owners of these enslaved Black people, that that fact by itself enhanced the dignity of those who were not owned! Comparing their freedom against the plight of the enslaved made them feel better about themselves.

In Olmstead's other book, *Journeys through the Seaboard Slave States*, Olmstead focused on ways to elevate civil discourse and contribute to the betterment of society. Although he detested the idea of human bondage, he was not alarmed when he learned that a Black man or woman was incapable of being educated, nor could they improve themselves to a condition where each could be more in control of their own lives. Even though Olmstead felt Blacks shouldn't be owned, he felt they were incapable of independence and required caretakers to survive.

Again, many people could not see the value of enslaved people. The racism and bigotry would soon come to a head, but for now, Olmstead's viewpoint would only "add more powder to the Keg."

13

The Bloody Build Up

"If you can dream it, you can do it." –Walt Disney.

Let me take a step back into 1628. Remember that this is 150 years earlier than the American Revolution. I need to share with you some things about John Winthrop. He was a lawyer and a Puritan leader of the first big wave of the Great Migration of British to America. He was the governor for 18 terms of the Massachusetts Bay Colony and expelled people for not following the harsh Puritan laws.

John Winthrop came to embody Puritan virtues and values (basically purifying Catholic elements they found offensive) and their intolerance for dissenting views. He was instrumental not only in establishing the colony and expanding it but for his written works, *A Model of Christian Charity* and *A Little Speech on Liberty*. These works, among others, defined the difference between *natural* and *civil* freedom. Winthrop was not kind to Native Americans and was a slave owner. He sold enslaved people and assisted in selling and transporting Pequots (a native American tribe) as slaves to other regions.

Winthrop's written work was a foundation for many United States presidents' thinking that America was a *beacon on a hill*. It was carried through the administrations of our first four presidents. How was he able to hold the light of liberty while enslaving others?

All groups have more things in common with other groups than you would think. Anne Hutchinson and Roger Williams in the seventeenth century did not believe they had a right to take lands and property from the Wampanoag, nor did these new settlers have any right to force the Wampanoag to accept their laws or their religion.

Anne Hutchinson was believed to be a threat to the church because she did not think new worshippers needed a minister to interpret the scriptures for themselves; they could receive the word of God themselves and not just accept dogma. She helped lead many on the path toward religious toleration.

Still, Puritans did not accept that women were equal to men and that those women could have a voice in society. Hutchinson challenged gender roles and expressed her voice in community religious matters. Men did not accept her voice.

At around the same time, John Winthrop won many arguments by stressing that he had authority because he was a man, not because his arguments were superior to others. If the Puritans failed to uphold their Covenant with God, their sins and errors would be exposed to the world, and they would fail to live up to their belief that they were chosen by God to be a shining example of purity and morality.

Winthrop was the first to express the concept of the *American Dream* in which life could be better, more affluent, and fuller for everyone, with each person having within themselves the opportunity to succeed and live an enriched life.

Winthrop also believed that man could ally himself with other men and form a bond. Winthrop expected that *the ol, man* who came to America to find a better future could see it within others. There was no mention of man or woman, White, Black, etc...

Each person came to America to succeed so they could find a better future together in this new land and help all others to survive. This was a hope; this hope came with liberty; this hope came with justice, and this hope came with equality. But again, the one thing that was a major flaw in his thought was that John Winthrop was a slave owner.

Let's jump ahead to 1789. Merrill Jensen wrote *The New Nation: A History of the US During the Confe, eration 1781-1789.* Merrill Jensen set the groundwork for evaluating our early government from a unique perspective. He offers the idea that true Federalists believed that the most significant gains of the Revolution were the independence of the thirteen states and the creation of a central government subservient to those states. The states were federated and helped to create a central government.

The group leaders from the First Continental Congress in 1775 were Samuel Adams, Patrick Henry, Richard Henry Lee, George Clinton, James Warren, Samuel Bryan, George Bryan, Elbridge Gerry, and George Mason.

They were narrow-minded thinkers and had no desire to put any control on themselves. They believed that the states could not be governed without the central government, but I don't know if their opinions could be classified as interference.

As the 1790s began, these very new *Americans* became romantics, believing that if every man had the right to vote, the very problem of society could be solved. They set themselves up to be counted as part of the *American aristocracy*. That meant more privilege for them but less freedom for the average person further down the ladder, except that idea dissolved as personal greed, the desire for wealth and power consumed them for most of our history. Over time, that would mean more privilege for them but less freedom for the average person, and they had no problem with that.

The Madison presidency was held with strong Federalist views. Federalists favored weaker state governments, a strong centralized government, the indirect election of government officials, longer-term limits for officeholders, and representative, rather than direct, democracy.

Madison was the 4th president of the United States when he declared war on Great Britain in 1812 because the British were seizing neutral ships and cargoes on the high seas. The War in 1812 was declared mainly over national honor.

Concurrently, Napoleon was waging war against England and all of Europe. America was trying to support both sides until the British seized all neutral ships and naval ships holding American sailors, as their own and their cargoes, on the high seas.

This is important because the war was back, bringing the concept of independence to the forefront of America's doorsteps again. This time we were defending *our* land. The British, fighting Napoleon in Europe, couldn't effectively defend Canada. To summarize, American troops failed in their attempted invasions as British troops and Canadian militia met them on the North American field of battle (on the land that would become Canada). Native American fighters were summoned by the British because they were concerned with their thin forces fighting on two continents. However, the United States fared better at the Battle of Lake Erie, which defeated British naval forces. It is important to note that in 1813 enslaved African Americans took advantage of this opportunity to advocate for their freedom during the war.

According to the National Park Service, during the summers of 1813 and 1814, 4,000-5,000 enslaved people left the United States to fight on the side of the British in the hopes of securing freedom and safe passage for themselves and their families to some other destination. The British had promised the Native Americans more freedom for their support against the Americans, but they never delivered on that promise.

The British established Fort Albion on Tangier Island off the coast of Virginia in the Chesapeake Bay in April 1814. Nearly 1,000 enslaved people found refuge at the site because the British had declared it *their* land; therefore, the slaves would be free.

The British were able to mount a naval blockade off the East Coast where "they invaded and burned" Washington and the White House in August 1814. First Lady Dolley Madison helped to rescue the Gilbert Stuart portrait of George Washington from the White House dining room before the British arrived and commenced their barrage.

Back in Europe, Napoleon had abdicated months earlier, and by 1814, the war was winding down. The battles had stopped the French threat. Peace talks had started shortly before the attack on Washington, and both sides reached a tentative agreement with the Treaty of Ghent in Belgium on December 24, 1814.

British troops attacking New Orleans were unaware of the peace deal, which still had to be ratified by both governments. On January 8, 1815, the American forces, led by General Andrew Jackson, routed the British troops at New Orleans.

Promises made are not always promises kept. It was recorded that American General Andrew Jackson promised freedom to the enslaved people who fought for his campaign. Still, they gained no independence even after the war and remained enslaved: one more lie. The U.S. Senate ratified the treaty on February 15, 1815.

Even on opposing sides, many fought for the same reason: freedom. African Americans played an essential part in many battles, such as the Battle of Lake Erie, the fighting around Baltimore, the bombardment of Fort McHenry (America's National Anthem came out of this battle), and the Battle of New Orleans. For nearly all African Americans who fought in this war, the promises made were not promises kept. Why were Black men willing to sacrifice everything for a country that did not treat them equally?

How can America continue to have a Constitution and a Bill of Rights if they are still not ensuring equality? Merrill Jensen believed that "no behavior was more responsible for the failure to deal properly with slavery than the entitlement that these men felt was their due."

Historically, the importation of enslaved people ended with the Act prohibiting the importation of enslaved people in 1808. Still, the domestic slave trade was alive and well in the slave states, and debates in Congress were heated and vicious about the Act because it remained the law of the land.

Then in 1821, a treaty was signed between the United States and Spain. Spain declined as a world power, and the United States purchased Florida for 5 million dollars. Spain was now separated from the US and its territories, but unfortunately, Florida applied to the union and was admitted as a slave state.

In the 1840s, the people of America started getting *Oregon Fever* because of Westward expansion. More slave states and free states were formed because of the expansion. As the westward movement continued, this proved a sour taste for Congress.

This pairing of enslaved people and free states started from the beginning. But now, with more land and population, tensions accumulated, and the strain weighed on America. But even with more and more land available, the tension continued to build.

According to the Constitution, "by including three-fifths of slaves [who had no voting rights] in the legislative apportionment, the Three-fifths Compromise provided additional representation in the House of Representatives for slave states compared to free states."

Now, the United States would face a vicious pattern. The Missouri Compromise was part of federal legislation and compromised northern attempts to completely prohibit slavery's expansion by admitting Missouri (1821) as a slave state. As part of the compromise, the admission of Maine (1820) as a free state was accompanied by Missouri's compromise to join the Union as a slave state. The battle was on.

Next came the admission of Texas (1845). Texas was free when it was a country, but now after the Mexican-American War (1846-1848), more northern-southern conflict occurred. The settled portion of Texas was an area rich in cotton plantations and was dependent on slave labor; the mountainous west was not hospitable to cotton or slavery so that it could remain out of the beginning of the fray.

To keep the balance, under the Compromise of 1850, California was admitted as a free state. California's admission also meant no slave state on the Pacific Ocean. To avoid creating a free state majority in the Senate, California agreed to send one pro-slavery and one anti-slavery senator to Congress—the mess continued!

The Missouri Compromise of 1820 was followed by the Kansas-Nebraska Act of 1854. These acts allowed White male settlers in the new territories to vote on whether they would allow for the extension of slavery. This meant that people could identify as pro-or-anti-slavery. The result of this was a term called "Bleeding Kansas."

The people on all sides of this controversial issue flooded the territory, trying to influence the vote in their favor. Rival territorial governments, election fraud, and disputes over land claims all contributed to the violence: fighting, mobbing, and murder, happened as a result of this law, and over 54 people were killed, all as a result of the battles.

Many wanted Kansas as a slave state to be paired with Minnesota. This fighting escalated through the 1850s. "When the admission of Minnesota proceeded unimpeded in 1858, the balance in the Senate ended. They would never again pair a free state with a slave state. Once Oregon was admitted into the Union in 1859, it sealed the deal that more free states would reign.

Most people of the time supported a small central government and strong state governments, so the federal government was much weaker than you might have expected. Enveloping all these changes was an ever-growing tension over the economy, as southern states firmly defended slavery and northern states advocated for a more industrial, slave-free market. Connecticut and other northeastern states were worried about the pace of growth and wanted to slow this down. Well, the southern states were infuriated. This scheme gave the federal government more control over land costs by creating scarcity. To them, the more money the central government made, the stronger it became, and the more it took rights away from the states to govern themselves. The debate was on.

The Webster-Hayne Debate, a series of unplanned speeches presented before the Senate between January 19th and 27th of 1830, debated the powers of the federal and state governments.

The debaters were Senator Daniel Webster of Massachusetts and Senator Robert Y. Hayne of South Carolina. At a time when the country was undergoing drastic changes, this debate encapsulated the essence of the growing tensions dividing the nation.

The Webster-Hayne debate, which again was just one section of this more significant discussion in the Senate, is traditionally considered to have begun when South Carolina Senator Robert Y. Hayne stood to argue against Connecticut's proposal, accusing the northeastern states of trying to stall the development of the West so that southern agricultural interests couldn't expand. Hayne was a great orator, filled with fiery passion and eloquent prose.

Massachusetts Senator Daniel Webster was eloquent, he was educated, he was witty, and he was staunch defender of American liberty. For the next several days, the men traded speeches that contemporaries of the time described as the greatest orations ever delivered in the Senate. Webster's definition of the *Constitution as for the People, by the People, an* answerable to the People would form one of the most enduring ideas about American democracy.

How would the United States exist as a strong nation if individual states could make laws that supersede the powers of the federal government? A strong central government unites the states, without which we would be a collection of nation-states all doing different things.

Senator Hayne favored states maintaining the right to overrule the federal government and ignore federal laws that infringed on a state's popular opinion, such as a southern state wanting to perpetuate the institution of slavery.

Senator Webster argued the federal government had to have overriding power to unify, solidify, and strengthen the country. This can be summarized with the question - how are we best governed and strengthened - by listening to the voice of many or the few?

But something else was brewing that would soon come to a head. The small (and I say that with sarcasm) back story of this is about an enslaved person—you may have heard about him. This enslaved person was taken into a free state and then returned to a slave state. He sued in court. He wanted his freedom because he had been taken into a free US territory where he would no longer be enslaved.

This man sued the state of Missouri and then appealed to the US Supreme Court. The US Supreme Court ruled that the enslaved person was not a US citizen of any state, perpetuating the continued division of the American people.

You would be correct if you guessed that this was the court case of Dred Scott v. Sandford.

This would be the final spark that lit the long fuse that would plunge the United States into its bloodiest part of history yet—the Civil War.

14

Abraham Lincoln

"A somebody was once a nobody who wanted to and did."
- John Burroughs

Abraham Lincoln was born in a one-room, backwoods cabin in Kentucky on February 12, 1809. Kentucky, at that time, was a slave state, and although Abraham Lincoln didn't see many enslaved people, he did begin to hear the debate about slavery. His family did not own slaves. They were opposed to the idea. His parents were strong opponents of slavery.

His earliest memories were of this home and a flash flood that once washed away the corn and pumpkin seeds he had helped his father plant. His father, Thomas Lincoln, a sturdy pioneer, had migrated from England to Massachusetts, married Nancy Hanks, and together they had three children: Sarah, Abraham, and Thomas, who died in infancy.

In 1816, Thomas Lincoln moved with his family to south-western Indiana. Soon he built a permanent cabin. Abraham helped to clear the fields and take care of the crops but disliked hunting and fishing as well as the poverty found on the Indiana frontier. The unhappiest period of his boyhood followed the death of his mother in the autumn of 1818. He was bereft without the warmth of his mother's love. Shortly after that, Thomas Lincoln brought home from Kentucky, a new wife for himself, and a new mother for the children. Sarah Bush Johnston Lincoln, a widow with children of her own, had energy and affection to spare. She became especially fond of Abraham and him of her. He afterward referred to her as his "angel mother," and she inspired his love of reading and learning. Many people criticized him for reading too much. Think about it: most people in the back woods where he grew up saw no purpose in reading and thought. They thought Mr. Lincoln was wasting his time. However, only a few people would not notice him when he was around because he was reading. Early in life, Lincoln had been something of a skeptic and freethinker. Lincoln loved learning and read any book he could get his hands on. Lincoln was fond of the Bible and knew it well. He also was fond of Shakespeare. He liked the works of John Stuart Mill, particularly *On Liberty*.

Abraham Lincoln was from a hard-working family. He stood six feet four inches tall which was very tall in those days. Because of his height, he was always noticed. He became known for his physical strength. In one incident, three men were preparing to move a chicken house using three poles to help them carry it. Lincoln walked over, picked it up, and moved it himself.

At age seventeen, he got a job on a ferry boat delivering farm produce from one side of the Mississippi River. He was free; the outdoors, the river, and the freedom of being part of it all without any constraints. He became sold on the idea of freedom. However, it was here on the river that Abraham Lincoln first witnessed the brutality of slavery. It impacted him personally, and that experience would stay with him throughout his lifetime.

In 1830, the Lincoln family moved to Illinois. When Lincoln was 21, he was especially noticed for the skill and strength with which he could wield an ax. He was good-natured, though somewhat moody, talented as a mimic and storyteller, and readily attracted friends. After he arrived in Illinois, having no desire to be a farmer, the ambitious Lincoln tried his hand at various occupations because he knew he wanted to do more with his life than physical jobs or guiding rafts down a river. He experienced different jobs after the river, such as a shopkeeper, postmaster, and surveyor. He even spent some time in the military, although he once said mosquitoes were the only thing he had ever fought.

Lincoln then studied the subject he was most interested in, the Law. He worked hard, and in 1836, he qualified to become a lawyer. He started a law firm in Springfield, Illinois. His years as a lawyer also earned him the reputation of being a good speaker and a hardworking, honest man.

To keep himself busy, he found it necessary to practice law in the capital and follow the court as it made the rounds of its circuit. The coming of the railroads, especially after 1850, made travel more accessible, and his practice became more lucrative.

After several years as a lawyer, Lincoln saw the needs of the people and developed a desire to run for political office. When Lincoln first entered politics, Andrew Jackson was president. Lincoln shared the sympathies that the Jacksonians professed for the common man but disagreed with the Jacksonian view that the government should be divorced from economic enterprise.

> "The legitimate object of government," he later said, "is to do for a community of people whatever they need to have done, but cannot do it all, or cannot do so well, for themselves, in their separate and individual capacities."

Lincoln lost his first campaign for Congress but won the second time he ran. This small position in the Illinois government allowed him to see how the government structure worked. He served in the state legislature for eight years. He was elected to Congress for one term as a Whig.

Lincoln worked his way up in the political arena and even started public speeches about various issues. The one issue that was becoming more and more popular in the debate was slavery. Lincoln opposed slavery and spoke about that issue regularly.

By the time he became prominent in national politics, about 20 years after launching his legal career, Lincoln had made himself one of the most distinguished and successful lawyers in Illinois. He was noted not only for his shrewdness and practical common sense, which enabled him always to see to the heart of any legal case, but also for his invariable fairness and utter honesty.

While residing in New Salem, he fell in love with Mary Todd. Her family belonged to the social aristocracy of the town. Some of them frowned upon her association with Lincoln; from time to time, he also doubted whether he could ever make her happy. On November 4, 1842, they got married.

They had four children, all boys. Lincoln left the upbringing of his children mainly to their mother, who was alternately strict and lenient in her treatment of them. The Lincolns had a mutual affectionate interest in the welfare of their boys, were fond of one another's a company and missed each other when apart, as existing letters show. Like most married couples, the Lincolns also had their domestic quarrels, which sometimes were hectic. During their early married life, she unquestionably encouraged her husband and served as a prod to his ambition.

In Lincoln's view, Illinois and the West desperately needed aid for economic development, and from the outset, he associated himself with the party of Clay and Webster, the Whigs. As a Whig member of the Illinois State Legislature, to which he was elected four times from 1834 to 1840, Lincoln devoted himself to a grandiose project for constructing with state funds a network of railroads, highways, and canals. While in the legislature, he demonstrated that he was no abolitionist opposed to slavery. In 1837, the legislature introduced resolutions condemning abolitionist societies and defending slavery in the Southern states as "sacred" by virtue of the federal Constitution. Lincoln refused to vote for the resolutions. Together with a fellow member, he drew up a protest that declared, on the one hand, that slavery was "founded on both injustice and bad policy" and, on the other, that "the promulgation of abolition doctrines tends rather to increase than to abate its evils."

During his single term in Congress (1847–49), Lincoln gave little attention to legislative matters as the lone Whig from Illinois. He proposed a bill for the gradual and compensated emancipation of enslaved people because it was to take effect only with the approval of the "free White citizens" of the district; it displeased abolitionists as well as slaveholders and never was seriously considered.

Along with other members of his party, Lincoln voted to condemn President Polk and the war while also voting for supplies to carry it on. At the same time, he labored for the nomination and election of the war hero Zachary Taylor. After Taylor's success at the polls, Lincoln expected to be named commissioner of the general land office as a reward for his campaign services. He was bitterly disappointed when he failed to get the job. Meanwhile, his criticisms of the war had not been popular among the voters in his congressional district. At age 40, frustrated in politics, he seemed to be at the end of his public career.

By 1854, the rules under the Missouri Compromise were ending. It was discussed and finally approved that the compromise excluded slavery from some western territories. Not all people supported that. Some slaveholders believed the Constitution provided for slave owners to have the right to take their property anywhere. Not everyone supported that—people disagreed! Some thought that slavery could just be limited to certain areas.

The revival of that thinking was strengthened by the Kansas-Nebraska Act of 1854 and the Fugitive Slave laws that soon followed. However, that view of enslaved people *as property* was supported after it was challenged in the issues surrounding the Dred Scott decision and its resolution in 1857.

Remember the facts of the case, as laid out in Chapter 13. Dred Scott, a Black man, was transported to a free state, Michigan, and he remained slave property. However, if that status changed, did his status as an enslaved person stay the same or change? He was in a free state. Why wouldn't he be free?

If enslaved people could be moved to a non-slave state and remain as enslaved people because their owner/master brought them across state lines, did that affect the status of slavery in that state? When his owner died, did his status change? Was he still enslaved? Would he get his freedom upon his owner's death?

Well, Dred Scott's owner did die. Seemingly, Dred Scott remained property. He remained an enslaved person. However, if that had changed, did his status as an enslaved person remain the same? He now was in a free state; why wasn't he free? Dred Scott thought that he was now entitled to his freedom. His wife agreed. He sought and hired an attorney, and the case proceeded to litigation.

The Court decided against Dred Scott, proclaiming that Dred Scott was still *property*. Our Constitution guaranteed liberty. The definition of the word *liberty* was innate and eternal, so the categorization of *slaves* as property was absurd.

Some believed slavery was criminal and just plain wrong and that slavery would never be permitted in free states.

Even as a logical thinker, Abraham Lincoln reacted disgustingly to the Dred Scott ruling. It spurred him into more political action by publicly speaking out against it. He carefully considered all sides of each issue. The values that he thought about often appeared in his writings and his speeches.

Eventually, Lincoln decided to run for the United States Senate. He and the other candidate (Stephan Douglas) held many debates across the state—most of them relating to slavery. Douglas, a Democrat, argued that the Republicans posed a dangerous threat to the Constitution. Lincoln had declared the nation could not survive if the slave state–free state division continued; Douglas claimed the Republicans aimed to destroy what the founders had created. This author believes what the Founders created was not worth a lot.

Lincoln stood firmly with the Union. He wanted to protect it at all costs, giving his famous *A House Divided* speech that follows; you can understand the logic and thinking as we move closer to the Civil War.

> A house divided against itself cannot stand. I believe
> this government cannot endure permanently half Slave
> and half Free. I do not expect the Union to be dis-
> solved—I do not expect the house to fall—but I do
> expect it will cease to be divided. It will become all one
> thing or all the other. Either the opponents of slavery
> will arrest the further spread of it and place it where
> the public mind shall rest in the belief that it is in the
> course of ultimate extinction: or its advocates will push
> it forward till it shall become alike lawful in all the
> States—old as well as new, North as well as South.

During that debate, Lincoln shed light to the entire country on his beliefs about slavery and race:

> I have no purpose, directly or indirectly, to interfere
> with the institution of slavery in the States where it
> exists. I believe I have no lawful right to do so and am
> not inclined to do so. I have no purpose in introducing
> political and social equality between the White and
> Black races. There is a physical difference between the
> two, which, in my judgment, will probably forever
> forbid their living together upon the footing of perfect
> equality. . . . I, as well as Judge Douglas, am in favor
> of the race to which I belong having the superior
> position. . . .

> [N]otwithstanding all this, there is no reason in the world why [Blacks are] not entitled to all the natural rights enumerated in the Declaration of Independence, the right to life, liberty, and the pursuit of happiness. I hold that he is as much entitled to these as the White man. . . . [I]n the right to eat the bread, without the leave of anybody else, which his own hand earns, he is my equal and the equal of Judge Douglas, and the equal of every living man.

When the results of the election for the U.S. Senate came, Lincoln lost. However, these debates introduced Lincoln to the country, and two years later, Lincoln was elected President of the United States.

If you ask people what they know about Abraham Lincoln, they will usually tell you that he was the President who ended slavery in our country. However, he did not begin his Presidency with this in mind. We read above about Lincoln's view that the *house was divided*.

We know that Abraham Lincoln was always against slavery. That is true. He knew the immorality of slavery, but as the President, he was not planning on ending it in the way it happened. He knew that slavery was a significant part of our country's economy and that people in the north and the south depended on it. The economy in the south was primarily based on growing cotton, and slavery allowed cotton to be grown and harvested quickly and profitably.

In the North, there were factories, and a large part of them produced clothing made from that cotton grown in the South. Slavery for the north and the south was as important as oil in today's world. Lincoln's battle was to expose the truth and immorality of it all, but Lincoln was also embroiled in the reality that slavery was still to be reckoned with.

For example, our country was expanding west, and Lincoln felt that slavery could remain in the states that already had it, but any new states that joined our country would have to ban slavery. It was a compromise he felt he had to commit himself to.

When Lincoln was elected President, the southern states were agitated. How could he have carried the majority because the fact was that very few southerners voted for him? Southerners knew Lincoln would destroy their way of life, so in response, many southern states decided to *secee* or leave the country.

The South wanted to break away from the United States just as the colonies broke away from Britain during the American Revolution. Abraham Lincoln believed the South or —that no state —could leave the union, which prompted the president to declare war against the southern states attempting to secede from the Union, and thus the Civil War began.

Our Constitution did not create a path for any state or states that opposed the federal government's actions to leave the union by secession, and the Constitution also had not provided a path for those seceded states to re-enter the union without penalties or concessions.

When the Civil War began, Lincoln believed it was not a war to end slavery but a war to keep our country together. However, Lincoln's views about the war changed after several years of fighting. The press of the day presented an obstacle that Lincoln had to consider for several days before he felt that he must respond.

When newspapers printed that Lincoln had misrepresented the reason for the deaths of so many in the battles of the Civil War,

Lincoln said that the founders of our government were responsible for the causes of the war. Lincoln said that "the Founders had too much public respect, which they thought they were entitled to enjoy." But Lincoln did not think so.

These few dozen men had refused even to consider that Blacks were equal to Whites, and subsequently, Lincoln declined to even consider new rules in favor of Whites and against Blacks.

The Constitution is an integral part of freedom and liberty. The rights to freedom and equality must be upheld. Therefore slavery must end. The Founders hadn't discussed it in any meaningful way in the seventy years since the Constitution was ratified.

Lincoln insisted that enslaved and free Blacks were entitled to that consideration because they were human, and each possessed human rights! They were born in the same way as everyone else. They were ALL equal.

Many disagreed, but our Constitution and our Declaration of Independence clearly stated that all of us are *create* *equal* and that all of us are *entitle* *to certain rights* and that these rights that we are entitled to are *inalienable*. These rights cannot be denied, changed, or removed. That is the truth of America!

This is an integral part of freedom and liberty that wasn't discussed in those seventy years since the Constitution was ratified and hasn't even been practiced in more than two hundred years since! This conflict happened in good times, and it happened in bad times. Slavery fundamentally changed America.

Lincoln began a personal revolution in this nation's history and influenced his thoughts based on his notes. He said that the Civil War was being fought to uphold the Constitution, connect the

Union created by that document, and hold up support for its inherent truth.

The ideas of that Union were meant to support, cherish, and hand down to each subsequent generation to follow. It didn't necessarily mean that the next generation had to perpetuate the thinking of the previous one. It could have its thoughts, but did those eleven states have the constitutional right to secede and did the American people have the constitutional right to allow them to return to the Union after the Civil War? Is that equality?

Lincoln was not perfect, just like the rest of us. When the war began, the north had many advantages, but one major disadvantage was military leadership. Many of the best military leaders then decided to help the southern states—not the northern states. Lincoln was forced to use military generals who had little experience and often were afraid to fight. As a result, the northern states, or the Union as it was called, suffered many major defeats.

Lincoln was very logical in his thinking, but his heart was very emotional, and he often suffered from personal depression. He usually coped with his depression, but the war made it nearly impossible. Lincoln was the military's commander in chief, and tens of thousands of his soldiers were being killed. He felt responsible and greatly saddened by their deaths.

Lincoln was very involved in the war. Unlike most presidents who listened to and received information from their advisors, Lincoln would spend time alone, reading and researching military tactics and strategies. He would spend time in the telegraph office to receive the messages sent from the battlefront. He would even go out onto the front lines of battle. One time he was almost shot.

With all the military issues Lincoln faced, he also had family issues. One of the more well-known issues was that his wife, Mary Todd, was slightly eccentric. She would sometimes get extremely angry and violent towards her husband. The public also criticized her for spending large amounts of money on personal items and home furnishings for the White House. In addition to dealing with his wife's issues, Lincoln also had to deal with the death of his young son. It was another very difficult time for the President.

Why weren't all United States residents declared equal, and why didn't that equality start from the beginning? Lincoln believed that no man could be thought of as property. How could we have assumed that property and liberty could be conflated together?

Setting property free was a concept that no one discussed. Why aren't all men and women free? How can any human own another human? Human rights are human rights, and they still must be considered human rights for all of us. After all, why weren't all of us considered equal in the 18th century?

Why haven't these ideas become a reality in the 21st century? These ideals that simply remain as ideals were never applied to reality—equality never became a reality! Those ideals did not end inequality and did not bring about any reaction to help citizens of this nation ensure that our government would become more stable and permanent. It did not serve to provide security or answer to the directives provided by the words in the Preamble to our Constitution.

Our Founding Fathers did not apply the principle of *equality* provided by the preamble. They declared certain rights eternal, but they did not adequately allow our posterity and us to perpetuate those ideas. However, they took the first step by their declaration of 1776. They permitted the acceptance of slavery, property rights, and the rights of all people to participate in our political system. We continue to do this even today! Still, they stripped more citizens of their right to access the ballot. How did that help?

So, how are the American people free? How can those free people stabilize this country, increase participation in its government operation, and maintain itself? How will we be able to pass on the best parts of this nation to our posterity?

We will need more than luck! We will need truth. There were over 500,000 freed Blacks after the Civil War, but they, as freed people, had no rights and could not participate in this nation in any way after the Civil War. And why is that war still referred to as a Civil War when it was never that? It should have been referred to as the War between the States! Why is toleration not a part of our national vocabulary today?

That is an integral part of freedom and liberty, but it wasn't discussed in the last seventy-plus years since the Constitution was ratified. It hasn't even been practiced in the two hundred years since! But it happened in good times and bad times. The press of the day presented an obstacle that Lincoln had to consider for several days before he felt that he had to respond.

Before he died, Lincoln oversaw the ending of the War between the States. Sure, he wrote the Emancipation Proclamation in 1863, which outlawed slavery in all those rebelling states and fundamentally changed America. The 10th Amendment says: "The powers not delegated to the United States by the Constitution, nor prohibited by it to the States are reserved to the States respectively, or to the people." It is a far stretch for states to think they can secede based on this amendment.

Lincoln began a personal revolution of this nation's history as it influenced his thoughts based on his thoughts and observations. He said that the War between the States was being fought to uphold the Constitution and the Union that the document was meant to support—asserting the final ruling that all men are created equal. The ideas of the Union written in that document were meant to help, maintain, and hand down to each subsequent generation that followed all of the ideals incorporated in our Constitution. It didn't necessarily follow that the next generation had to perpetuate the thinking of the previous one.

Think about it. The Founders, only 80 years earlier, created this War. How? They had three major issues to solve during the First Constitutional Convention in 1787:

1) Should *enslave* *people* count as part of the population?

2) Abolishing the slave trade, and

3) if an enslaved person escaped to freedom, is that state obligated to return the enslaved person to their "owner"?

All three of these were the Great Compromise. Well, when you compromise with human beings, war will be the result. The War, *the conflict* which began in 1787, had actually just been experienced again from 1861-1865 because nothing had been resolved with the previous conflict. All major values and ideals had been left unresolved in the ensuing years.

At long last, that bloody battle had been won for enslaved people to become free! However, it would take generations to change people's way of thinking that all are created equal.

Since his death, Abraham Lincoln has done more for the United States of America than any other president in its history. He alone understood his oath to preserve, protect, and defend the Constitution. He used his executive authority to help level the playing field and ensure that all human lives matter.

Again, the formerly enslaved Black people were at least free according to the 13th Amendment. The law had been passed, yet it would take generations for people to accept those changes and allow freedom to reign, mainly because it is so connected with hate, power, control, war, and bloodshed. Time would prove a little more challenging for certain portions of the United States to fully accept it.

President Lincoln believed that in times of war, as President, he was responsible for the well-being and survival of the nation. He had to find the path to "preserve the Union, oversee the vindication of democracy, and the death of slavery. Lincoln's accomplishments would have ended very differently with a lesser man in the Oval Office, and America would have paid a very high price.

History is a witness to his ability to energize and mobilize the nation by remembering its best ideals while having no malice towards anyone. Lincoln pursued a "more perfect, more just, and more enduring Union."

The crisis of pitting brother against brother and the shedding blood over freedom and the equality of all humanity was fought between 1861-1865. Over 600,000 Americans lost their lives in the War between the States, and Lincoln witnessed the deep sorrows of those deaths, which produced heartaches, yet, he understood his duty. He never flinched or shirked from that duty and kept the union together.

No President has ever accomplished as much as Lincoln did. Let's remember that the most critical question still exists, WAS THE WAR JUSTIFIED?

Andrew Johnson took control of Reconstruction after Lincoln's death, and most in Congress expected him to maintain the same ideals as Lincoln. He first followed a harsh policy toward the defeated Southerners, denying political rights to anyone who supported the Confederacy in a military or governmental role, and agreed to arrest several prominent Confederate officials.

Johnson, however, did not want to punish all Southerners for the Civil War and only blamed wealthy and powerful planters. Johnson wanted to reunite the nation as quickly as possible while punishing the rebellion's leaders. He granted political rights to all Southerners who swore allegiance to the United States except wealthy landowners and Confederate officials. Those Southerners that Johnson excluded from political rights could attain them by seeking a pardon directly from him. In late 1865, Johnson pardoned hundreds of applicants daily; he granted pardons to roughly 90 percent of those who asked for them. By December 1865, Johnson also had allowed 10 of the 11 seceded states back into the Union. His only conditions were that the states adopt a constitution that repudiated secession, acknowledged the end of slavery, and repudiated any debts the states had entered into during the Civil War.

Johnson's actions angered the Radical Republicans in Congress they interpreted as undermining the Reconstruction and refused to allow Southern representatives and senators to take their seats in Congress.

In 1866, Congress passed the Civil Rights Bill, which granted African Americans equal protection under the law, and renewed the Freedmen's Bureau that same year. President Johnson vetoed both of these bills, but Congress overturned both vetoes. Johnson was accused of "attempting to return Black Americans to a 'condition only less wretched that the slavery from which the war for the Union had rescued' them" (Szalai, 2021).

The first action that the Republican majority took was to enact the First Reconstruction Act despite Johnson's veto. This act split the South into five districts. In each district, soldiers of the United States would enforce martial law. To gain admittance to the Union, Congress required Southern states to draft new constitutions guaranteeing African-American men the right to vote. The constitutions also had to ratify the Fourteenth Amendment, which granted African Americans equal protection under the law. In effect, Congress rejected Johnson's plan for Reconstruction and implemented a much harsher policy toward white Southerners.

15

Extending the Franchise To Women; Voting in America

"Women belong in all places where decisions are being made. It shouldn't be that women are the exception."- Ruth Bader Ginsburg.

Women have a foundational place in the tapestry of history. Without women, where would we be? Without women, from where would our children have come? It takes women who are not driven by their egos and not limited by their thoughts about money to create a just world for the next generation. Women have been the foundation to which humanity owes its very existence.

To illustrate my point, let's talk about the very fabric of America. If you know anything about tapestry, you know there are interlocking woven textiles. This is fabric and, for our purposes, the structure of tapestries. Tapestries consist of two main components: the warps and the wefts. The warps are the foundational threads of yarn, wool, or linen fiber. After they are set and stretched, the weft is woven in. Wefts are the colored thread that interlocks between the warps.

Women are the warps in our lives. They are the foundational piece of the tapestry, but just like the warp in a tapestry, they largely remained unnoticed, and yet without them, nothing could be woven.

Now, if America's fabric is to be adequately woven, it is time to extend the franchise of equality to women. I must talk about the history of some essential fabric of the lives of our women. Please note that this is only a snapshot of the tapestry, but I know these women were key in starting the conversation and getting the world to pay attention to women's rights and equality. Their voices must be heard.

At this point in history, I must share a little history of Mary Wollstonecraft (1759-1797). Wollstonecraft is best known for *A Vin•ication of the Rights of Woman* (1792), in which she argues that women *are not* naturally inferior to men but appear to be only so because they *lack e•ucation.* In fact, they were denied an education by men throughout most of human history. Mary Wollstonecraft had a view of God similar to the enlightenment view of the social questions of the day. She suggests that men and women should be treated as *rational beings* and imagines a social network founded on reason. Wollstonecraft's work was unique in suggesting that the betterment of women's status would be effected through such political change as the radical reform of national educational systems. Mary stated, "Such change would benefit all society."

Think about it, for centuries, women were denied an education simply because they were looked at as the inferior sex, and as such, they had no rights but one: to be everything they could be for the men in their lives. That meant providing for children, caring for their husbands, and meeting the demands placed upon her.

Women were the guardian of light in that endeavor of family and nurturing. Unfortunately, looking at the fabric of America for centuries, were to stay only at home and could not participate in any affairs outside the home.

> Wollstonecraft (unlike many other voiceless women) used her voice! She stated "that educated mothers would benefit the commonwealth in three ways:
> (1) by modeling patriotism for their children;
> (2) by demonstrating a love of humanity that subsequently reinforced the lasting bonds of camaraderie necessary for civil society; and
> (3) by inculcating children with "public spirit."

Children with educated mothers are empowered to make better choices and can fulfill their most significant potential. If America's fabric included what women had hoped to do for America, just think about how a *Secon Chance* could have promoted the change we all wish we always had, which would have imbued our society with egalitarian principles.

With education comes an awareness of one's duty to society and the functioning of a democracy. Voting is part and parcel of this duty, and voting is a right because of free speech. The words supposedly protect free speech in the Declaration of Independence, and those words were repeated in our Constitution. You can look for yourselves. It is right there; this democracy is a participating form of government.

Some among us may try to stifle women from talking, but no one can stop women from thinking. All people must be allowed to express their own opinions. We can try to persuade others to accept the premises of our thoughts. This entire process is integral to the concept of democracy.

Let's look back at the election of 1788. This is the first election for the president's office in the United States of America. There weren't many problems with voting because all votes were cast at the Constitutional Convention. Well, there was only one candidate, and that was George Washington. In addition to that, only men were allowed to vote. All the people who were voting were sitting at the convention. There was absolute certainty about the vote. Everyone knew it. The point was that there was only one candidate, so only one outcome was possible.

What about in the 1792 election? Were women a part of the franchise yet? No! The voting situation was a little different because there were now two candidates. When it came time for the election, the people had a choice of when to vote because the election began on November 2nd, 1792, and closed on December 5th, 1792. That action extended the franchise from less than a hundred voters to more than 28,000 voters, and more than a month was provided so that everyone who wanted to vote could— except for women, Blacks, and other minorities.

Just to note, in the second presidential election of 1792, we had only 6.3% of the population in the United States voting out of a population of more than two million. Those early colonists trusted themselves but did not trust the many other residents of early America.

Our second president, John Adams, said that "immigrants [Blacks and women] know little about this country. Why should they participate in our elections?" In my opinion, I feel that this idea still happens today in the 21st century.

Soon things would change. In 1792, Sarah Grimke was born, and in 1805 her sister, Angelina, was born. Things would not be so quiet anymore. Their father, John Faucheraud Grimké, a head judge of the state supreme court in South Carolina, denied his daughters an education just because they were not men—because they were another gender. Ergo, they were inferior.

Sarah and Angelina were fortunate because they had a younger brother, Thomas. Unbeknownst to their father, Thomas helped to educate his sisters, even though their father had forbidden him from doing just that.

The sisters Grimke spoke about human bondage; they thought about the north and how life was different from what they were experiencing where they lived. They thought about William Lloyd Garrison, an abolitionist, and his newspaper, *The Liberator*.

The Liberator featured a letter, one that Angelina and Sarah had penned. Garrison read what they wrote and personally responded to them. Angelina and Sarah were sympathetic to the ideas Garrison was writing about in his paper. Many enthusiastic audiences read his words from the northern states. These readers were part of an increasingly sympathetic audience, but these were people who could not vote.

They were trying to get their voices heard, but they could find no path. Such was the case of Mary Murray back in the 1770s. She was another woman lost in the tapestry of America but played a vital role in winning the war. Possibly, dare I say, Mary was another *slave* to the fabric of history. Her heroism in Chapter 9 must be told to all generations.

I must say that with the pervasive concepts of slavery and a lack of equal rights for women in the 17th, 18th, and 19th centuries in

America, it's no wonder that people had to take matters into their own hands. Women understood what is right and moral so much that I must mention the following three women. These women lived in or captured the horrors of slavery.

The Underground Railroad was one such act. It had to be created because we are talking about humanity. People are humans; therefore, all of us are entitled to the rights claimed in the Bill of Rights and the Constitution.

Despite the changes that well-meaning people brought about, the 19th century is not considered one of our most acceptable centuries.

One woman, Sojourner Truth, had her journey to tell. She assumed the name of Sojourner Truth when she escaped slavery in 1826. She was armed and ready with the phrase, "truth is powerful, and it must prevail." She encouraged Black Americans to stand up for their universal right to liberty.

The truth was later able to meet President Lincoln and share her activism for the abolitionist movement with him. She talked of an acceptable quality of life for all. She also said that the words *voting* and *restrictions* should not even appear in the same sentence! Voting should be that right held by every human being.

Another formerly enslaved person, Harriet Tubman, also knew all of this. She braved the Underground Railroad not only once but successfully brought over 300 enslaved Black people to freedom.

Harriet, of her journey, said, "When I crossed the line from Southern States which had their slaves, into the North, where I witnessed that these citizens did not own slaves and had started the Underground Railroad to fight the fugitive slave

> laws which permitted slave owners to cross into the northern
> states to capture these Blacks; even if they could not provide
> proof of that ownership, I felt like I was in Heaven."

New patriots like Harriet Beecher Stowe brought clarity to these severe realities of slavery when she exposed the harsh conditions under which innocent Black people were forced to live without any control of their lives or destiny. Her book, *Uncle Tom's Cabin,* highlighted the evils of slavery, angered the slaveholding South, and inspired pro-slavery copycat works in defense of the institution of slavery. Later, this became the basis for the movement that led to the Equal Rights Amendment.

The women I've mentioned above played a part in bringing up hard conversations like slavery and voting in the 19th century. Women were trying to make the world safe for human differences at that time.

Women were trying to obtain the right to vote. They were considered guilty because the voting laws were limited, only giving men the right to vote.

Why did this happen? How could it happen in America? It is simply because men wrote these laws, and men observed them. Not only that, but no one considered what happened through the administration of those laws that prevented women from being able to use the ballot. Women were not even asked their opinion about this.

If this is the case, let's now get to the other side of history, shall we? Many of you know the names of Susan B. Anthony and Elizabeth C. Stanton. They were the women who gathered a nation's strength and movement for women's rights. What did they contribute to America?

Let me share about Susan B. Anthony. She was born on February 15, 1820, to Daniel Anthony, a cotton mill owner, and his wife, Lucy Read Anthony. They were a Quaker family who came from Massachusetts.

Susan B. Anthony was raised to be independent and outspoken. She grew up in a politically active family who worked to end slavery as part of the abolitionist movement. Her parents, like many Quakers, believed that men and women should study, live and work as equals and commit themselves equally to the eradication of cruelty and injustice in the world.

When the family moved to Rochester, New York, in 1845, Anthony's social circle opened up and included anti-slavery activist Frederick Douglass. The latter would later join Anthony in the fight for women's rights, along with William Lloyd Garrison. The rights of the oppressed people were now coming to the forefront.

Something interesting to note was that Susan B. Anthony was also part of the temperance movement, which attempted to cease the production and sale of alcohol in the United States. She became a temperance activist in Rochester, NY, and believed drinking alcohol was a sin and that male drunkenness was harmful to innocent women and children who suffered from the poverty and violence it caused.

Holding this viewpoint was a massive challenge because Susan B. Anthony found that few politicians took her anti-liquor crusade seriously. Why? Because she was a woman and because she was advocating on behalf of a *women's issue.* Why was drunkenness a women's issue? Women were not drinking and causing poverty—the men were!

Susan knew that this was going to damage her real push to try to win the vote. She knew that if women could vote, and hold office, then laws could be changed, and temperance could be addressed. She wanted to ensure that the government kept women's interests in mind. So voting became the more significant cause.

Another incredible but different woman came into the scene during Susan B Anthony's work. Her name was Elizabeth Cady. She was born in Johnston, NY, on November 12, 1815.

Unlike Anthony, Cady was born into privilege; her father was an "owner of enslaved workers, a prominent attorney, a Congressman, and a judge who exposed his daughter to the study of law and other so-called male domains early in her life. This exposure ignited a fire within Cady to seek a remedy to the unjust law and how they referred to women.

A man named Henry Brewster Stanton introduced Elizabeth Cady to the abolitionist movement. He was a journalist and abolitionist volunteering for the American Anti-Slavery Society. Elizabeth Cady married Henry Stanton but insisted that the word *obey* be dropped from the marriage vows.

The Stantons had six living children, and Elizabeth had the opportunity to be a part of the convention held in Seneca Falls, NY, in 1848. This convention was the turning point in establishing the equality of voting for women and men; this was sixty years after the Constitution had promised to deliver equal voting.

At that convention, Elizabeth Cady Stanton helped write the Declaration of Sentiments, a document modeled after the Declaration of Independence. According to the research, this document laid out how men had oppressed women in the following ways:]

- preventing them from owning land or earning wages
- preventing them from voting

- compelling them to submit to laws created without their representation
- giving men authority in divorce and child custody proceedings and decisions
- preventing women from gaining a college education
- preventing women from participating in most public church affairs
- subjecting women to a different moral code than men
- aiming to make women dependent and submissive to men

Stanton read the *Declaration of Sentiments* at the convention, and sixty-eight women and thirty-two men signed it—including Frederick Douglass. Some withdrew their names, and the pressure mounted, but Stanton had caught fire and knew she must stand for women's voting rights.

Until that day at the convention, our nation had grown under nine presidents who served their terms without considering the concept of equality and advancing the idea of women having an equal right to vote as men!

As stated before, women had no property rights in those early days. Men believed women were incapable of being competent and thought that if they couldn't reason, how could they vote?

In 1848 at the Seneca Falls Convention, Elizabeth Cady Stanton and Lucretia Mott met and argued. They argued about the path forward. They believed that women should not be held back from education and, therefore, should not be held back from voting. However, men refused to discuss women's right to vote or even discuss it.

This convention launched the path to suffrage for women. In 1851, Susan B. Anthony and Elizabeth Cady Stanton met. They were vastly different, but they were fast friends. Anthony traveled the country speaking and Stanton, due to her family duties, used her words and pen to fight the fight. The focus was on women's suffrage and the overall rights of women.

In fact, according to research, Stanton's 1854 address to the legislature of New York "helped secure reforms passed in 1860 which allowed women to gain joint custody of their children after divorce, own property and participate in business transactions." Now that's some change!

Both women joined the Women's Loyal National League to encourage Congress when the Civil War broke out. This group supported passing the 14th and 15th amendments. Black men, through the 13th Amendment, were free, and through the 15th Amendment, they were given the right to vote, but alas—no voting rights for women—yet!

Why was that? Men needed women to start families and raise their children, which kept them from considering that women had a right to participate. Women asked *why* men should be able to vote when women were prohibited from doing so. The movement involving pursuing voting rights fell into an abyss.

Lucy Stone was an early advocate of anti-slavery and women's rights. She was born in Massachusetts and was the first woman to graduate from Oberlin College in 1847. Lucy began lecturing for the anti-slavery movement as a paid agent for the American Anti-Slavery Society. Other women noticed and also took up the fight.

Lucy Stone said in 1847, "I expect to plead not for the enslaved person only, but for suffering humanity everywhere. Especially, do I mean to labor for the elevation of my sex."

As a point of interest, Lucy did not participate in the Seneca Falls Convention, but she was an organizer of the 1850 Worcester First National Woman's Rights Convention.

She spoke at the National Woman's Rights Convention in Syracuse, New York, which is credited for converting Susan B. Anthony to the cause of women's rights.

There is power in anyone seeking the truth and trying to do what is right.

Lucy Stone kept her maiden name when she was married and continued the fight for voting rights. She also joined Stanton and Anthony as an abolitionist and a suffrage activist.

Stanton, Anthony, and Stone fought to achieve the vote for women. They fought for the right to vote up until their deaths. Unfortunately, they all died well before the 19th Amendment was passed and had to entrust their work to thousands of others to carry the torch until the goal was obtained.

Women getting the freedom to express themselves through the franchise had to wait until August 18, 1920, under President Woodrow Wilson. However, that is only half of the story.

Alice Paul was another excellent advocate for women's voting and helped secure passage of the 19th Amendment to the United States Constitution, granting women the right to vote. Alice was the oldest of four children and was raised by a mother, Tacie, who fought for gender equality, education for women, and working to improve society.

Alice Paul's mother, Tacie, a suffragist, brought her daughter with her to women's suffrage meetings. She was bitten by the bug but knew she must first obtain as much education as possible. She did. She graduated with a biology degree and a master's degree, and as she studied in London for her Ph.D., she met another American named Lucy Burns, who helped her be a huge voice to continue the fight for the right to vote.

Long story short, Alice Paul knew how to fight. And she had quite a fight against President Wilson. Wilson thought the women he encountered in this fight were insulting, unfeminine, and unpatriotic.

Alice Paul knew that, so she organized marches and rallies and then created a group called the "Silent Sentinels," who picketed for 18 months in front of the White House with signs that read, "Mr. President, how long must women wait for liberty?"

Alice Paul was jailed for seven months and performed a hunger strike. News of this hit the press, and the pressure was on President Wilson to give in. He had been cornered, and so he caved.

When the amendment was approved, granting women the right to vote, an overwhelming majority agreed. By that event, 20 million American women won the right to vote.

Look at our story! It should not be referred to as *his* story; it should always be portrayed as *Our* Story.

Another incredible woman was Margaret Mead, a cultural anthropologist. She believed and taught that children learn from watching adults behave. This was a part of the nature versus nurture argument.

It made a point when it advanced the concept that motherhood serves to reinforce male and female gender roles in all societies. Beyond that, they offered that families are created by women and held together by those same adults, starting at the first sign of motherhood.

Anthropologists believe that the first sign of civilization begins with the all-important concept of addressing the idea of considering what each person requires and then addressing those needs with compassion.

Ruth Benedict, another anthropologist who studied with Margaret Mead, added that "the purpose of anthropology was to make the world safe for human differences."

Aren't compassion and empathy the primary concepts that we learn from culture?

So America, the question is, what is the culture that you want to leave for the next generation?

Women have endured such a long road and fight for equality and freedom. But they do it. They never quit! They find ways to fight and carry the banner, bring awareness, make and change laws, and bring hope and light to many in darkness—and the fight continues.

16

Racial Injustice Has Deep Roots

"To bring about change, you must not be afraid to take the first step. We will fail when we fail to try."
– Rosa Parks

The Farewell of a Virginia Slave Mother
By John Greenleaf Whittier

> GONE, gone,—sold and gone,
> To the rice-swamp dank and lone.
> Where the slave-whip ceaseless swings,
> Where the noisome insect stings,
> Where the fever demon strews
> Poison with the falling dews,

Where the sickly sunbeams glare
Through the hot and misty air;
Gone, gone—sold and gone,
To the rice-swamp dank and lone,
From Virginia's hills and waters;
Woe is me, my stolen daughters!
GONE, gone,—sold and gone,
To the rice-swamp dank and lone.
There is no mother's eye near them,
There is no mother's ear that can hear them;
Never, when the torturing lash
Seams their back with many a gash,
Shall a mother's kindness bless them,
Or a mother's arms caress them.
Gone, gone—sold and gone,
To the rice-swamp dank and lone,
From Virginia's hills and waters;
Woe is me, my stolen daughters!
GONE, gone,—sold and gone,
To the rice-swamp dank and lone.
Oh, when weary, sad, and slow,
From the fields, at night they go,
Faint with toil, and racked with pain,
To their cheerless homes again,
There no brother's voice shall greet them;
There no father's welcome meet them.
Gone, gone—sold and gone,
To the rice-swamp dank and lone,
From Virginia's hills and waters;
Woe is me, my stolen daughters!
GONE, gone,—sold and gone,
To the rice-swamp dank and lone.

From the tree whose shadow lay
On their childhood's place of play;
From the cool spring where they drank;
Rock, and hill, and rivulet bank;
From the solemn house of prayer,
And the holy counsels there;
Gone, gone—sold and gone,
To the rice-swamp dank and lone,
From Virginia's hills and waters;
Woe is me, my stolen daughters!
GONE, gone,—sold and gone,
To the rice-swamp dank and lone.
Toiling through the weary day,
And at night the spoiler's prey.
Oh, that they had earlier died,
Sleeping calmly, side by side,
Where the tyrant's power is o'er,
And the fetter galls no more!
Gone, gone—sold and gone,
To the rice-swamp dank and lone,
From Virginia's hills and waters;
Woe is me, my stolen daughters!
GONE, gone,—sold and gone,
To the rice-swamp dank and lone.
By the holy love He beareth;
By the bruised reed He spareth;
Oh, may He, to whom alone
All their cruel wrongs are known,
Still, their hope and refuge prove,
With more than mother's love.
Gone, gone—sold and gone,
To the rice-swamp dank and lone,

From Virginia's hills and waters;
Woe is me, my stolen daughters!

Unfortunately, that mother's pain rang true for thousands of mothers. Remember that even with the 13th Amendment, it would take generations of time for people to think and change their hearts to accept the new law. America, this happened on your watch, and what was to be done?

Paul Bohannan, an anthropologist, pointed out that Black people looked different from White people and what White people provided as much heritage to the new American continent as any other group. I disagree. I think Black people worked longer and harder than White settlers and received little reward for their efforts.

A French trader noticed this. He believed that the Blacks worked tirelessly and thought that they received little reward for those efforts. No one noticed.

These Blacks arrived in the colonies with some awareness of what was happening in their world. They learned about survival. They possessed dignity, and that propped up their sense of pride. They worked longer, but the time and effort they spent completing their tasks were not appreciated. They had to support their families. They ignored the slight and just went back to work.

People came to this country as indentured servants. They were willing to give up a part of their freedom to achieve transportation to America. Many others came to America simultaneously, and these people had Black skin, but they were still human, even if people brought them here as enslaved people. The Whites, who worked there, were part of a larger group and assumed control, ignoring what was happening with the minority Blacks.

> Immanuel Kant states, "the sole feature that gives any specific action any moral worth is that the outcome achieved by that action is based upon the motive that inspires the action itself."

Thus, the passage of the 13th Amendment after the Civil War freed the enslaved people, and the 14th Amendment, which followed it, were rights granted to Americans regarding the principle of equality. That is, citizenship came with rights, and formerly enslaved people were citizens and equal before the law, and that was what entitled all men and women to exercise the franchise equally.

We must slow down. We need to retrace steps that we overlooked. Most of the story was never presented by teachers in our schools. Most of the story was glossed over.

This is the *Secon‍ Chance* that this book affords the reader because of the many past opportunities never discussed or considered relevant to the curriculum that each local school board presented to their students. The residents (citizens) didn't object to the curricula that the school boards had mandated to be taught in the schools that most of us attended but never learned much from.

They did not teach this part of American History because no one ever mentioned the true story to them. Perhaps these issues were never considered, or maybe these issues were not regarded as appropriate.

Blacks have been on this continent for more extended periods than White settlers. Black people have been in America going back at least 3,000 years. That is a more extended period than Whites. Before these early settlers came to this continent, they had families and rights and deserved to be treated with dignity and respect like all other humans.

Fast forward to now; we have the Thirteenth, Fourteenth, and Fifteenth Amendments. They have been part of the Constitution for more than 160 years. They promised equality. Lincoln said these rights were inherited from the glory days and now had finally come to pass. This happened via the law, but it takes generations to change their biased and bigoted hearts to conform to that change.

With the passage of the 15th Amendment, all these *equal* citizens obtained the right to vote! This fact made each citizen similar to everyone else, or so it seemed.

When slavery ended, many of the enslaved people went west. They settled in rural communities in areas that were called territories; these territories were not yet part of the United States. The residents of these territories included many Native American tribes who possessed large tracts of land, as they had for generations. Included in this group were members of the Seminole Nation and the Kiowa. Remember that these people living there then were only twenty-five years removed from enacting the Civil War amendments.

These people were residing side-by-side in areas that would one day become the state of Oklahoma. To add to this mix, thousands of White Southerners who grew up in slavery moved to these territories along with the many Black people who had come here after the war because of the Homestead Act of 1862.

This western territory, in what would become Oklahoma, was before them. White slave owners who teemed into these areas cajoled many Black settlers into selling their recently acquired lands cheaply. These White Southerners schemed, lied, and misrepresented what they planned to do in Oklahoma. Many Blacks feared for their lives.

These Blacks who inhabited these lands could not read or write. They were just there to be taken advantage of by the invading White hordes; they were not disappointed. Before these Southern Whites poured into the territory, there was growing equality, squelched by the force of the White mobs who soon arrived.

These Whites pillaged Black homesteads and raided and stole their planting fields, taking their crops. These Whites burned down hovels and interrupted whatever these itinerant drudges had built for themselves so they could cling to life. The Blacks could barely find an opportunity to maintain whatever energy they had created. Soon most of that life was taken away from them.

Whites thought that these newly freed Blacks, residing alongside them, did not deserve to be free because they were Black, and the Whites considered themselves superior. These were desperate times. The United States, a neighbor of these territories, had many citizens, but America would not offer assistance.

In the ensuing years, Whites sent delegations to Washington D.C. seeking an *appointment* to discuss statehood in the United States of America for their Oklahoma. Theodore Roosevelt was happy to propose statehood for Oklahoma. He provided these delegations with an application for statehood. Soon Oklahoma became our newest state. However, the events near Tulsa and Norman created a lingering scar.

Edmund Burke once said, "too many good men have done nothing."

Many of us, even presidents, could have done better if we had stopped thinking about ourselves. They might have thought about the people of this country who made up the various parts of the electorate in the nation that they were leading. That never happened then and hasn't changed much until now. Would that have been too much to ask - for people to think of others instead of only themselves?

White women did not get a chance to participate, and Black women were far back in line. None of the women were offered rights of participation and had no seats at the table. Black women had no voice because they had two strikes against them; their sex and skin color.

These Black females were permitted to have children but were denied a role in their democracy, the democracy in which they lived. They were offered no education or freedom of speech and couldn't read or write. They could not assemble in groups anywhere without the police accompanying them.

This was a White man's role in a White man's world; females were treated like chattel, not people. Many believed it was against the sanctity of human nature for women to be permitted to speak in public. The women could watch and listen from afar in the spectator galleries but could not participate. Even the male abolitionists objected to women speaking in public.

The ideals of our Constitution were denied then to half our population; all women and all Blacks. This was indeed an injustice. Never forget that White people are the only group who invented the concept of *race* first! The *know-nothings* gained a foothold in those times. They stood firm against offering rights and Constitutional changes to new Americans because they were fiercely anti-immigrant and anti-catholic.

The *know-nothings* were against anyone who wasn't them. If you were foreign-born, you were not their friend. They feared that formerly enslaved people would take their jobs, preventing them from earning a livelihood. No foreigners were given a seat at the table, and no White citizens would even consider offering a seat to anyone who didn't look like them.

The KKK, the most influential hate group in American history, attacked and burned thousands; they destroyed homes and farms, wiping out the hopes of many new immigrants who thought differently than them and didn't measure up to what White people expected.

Soon the Knights of the White Camellia, another political terrorist group, gained traction in the American South toward the end of the nineteenth century. They supported White supremacy and opposed rights for Blacks, women, and formerly enslaved people.

Harper Lee wrote the drama *To Kill a Mockingbir* (1960) to highlight racism and intolerance in the post-Civil War South. I've tried to find good stories about the people who lived in this period but have come up empty. A military memo reportedly said, "although Black men were citizens of the United States, most White Americans regarded these Black men as being *inferior beings.*"

Military personnel was advised to avoid eating with or shaking hands with these Black soldiers because "you might spoil them!" Further, it was believed that White officers should not extend respect to Black officers! That was true even if you had fought and lived together or eaten meals alongside each other because they didn't look the same.

I am of the opinion that if this idea has ever been witnessed in this country, no one who comes across this concept has even thought of addressing it or trying to rectify it! These sins have simply been brushed under the rug. When has this nation sought to improve the relationships between Whites and Blacks?

As charitable humans, we don't consider our stories contradictions. We are all living together, but not really. Many White people have never attempted to alleviate this pain by offering an open hand to Blacks. Why is that so difficult? We don't need second-class citizenship for anybody. That concept should be easy to accept.

We all have stories that we tell ourselves about our family, our private jokes, and what makes our family different from every other family. All of this leads to a feeling of warmth and trust. All families may do this, but they don't often extend that same compassion and courtesy to other families, who ultimately want very similar things out of life. Why don't we do that?

You were trying to say something, and others expressed the evidence of that truth. Every family has qualities that make that family unique. We learn how to create a moral identity specific to each of us. No one has authority in these situations. What matters is that you can decide the truth as you believe it.

Once other opinions are articulated and each draws some support, we must make a choice and are at a critical juncture. Now, we are facing a choice. This is democracy; here, we will witness the working parts of the concept, which we call majority rule. How do the thoughts and opinions of various people become so ingrained?

As people share their ideas and opinions, no matter how biased or exclusionary they are, those ideas and opinions become part of the common truth from which laws and customs are created. Herein lies the dilemma. We like to seek commonality among ourselves. It's easy to talk to people who share your opinion, but what about those who differ from you? How do we listen to both sides of the story to understand each person's viewpoint without devolving into anger, contention, and shouting matches?

There are different versions of History, and people sometimes fail to understand how to get to an agreement with one another. Here is where we must find the everyday tool that we can use to articulate our reasoning processes. That tool is education.

The goal is a community, and the only way to achieve that goal is to speak with others, share a wide range of opinions and attempt to coalesce those opinions into an inclusionary majority. A majority can be formed and passed on with common agreement between participants through facts and emotional experiences. What you go through together and the stories that must be told are rooted in the complexities of each day.

Emma Goldman (June 1869 - August 1940) said, "the most violent element in society is ignorance." She meant that humans had to discover the roots of empathy and must not give up searching for it. She also said that we must understand each other before we can forgive each other.

Emma Goldman was considered to be an *anarchist.* Many people believed her to be an opponent of the established order thinking of her against all authority. They believed her to be someone who would adopt any means, even violent ones, to give vent to what she believed. Although she never gave any indication that this was true. She was labeled this way because she spoke vehemently about what she objected to, namely the denigration and holding back of women by men seeking to maintain their stronghold on American laws and customs. They slandered her in an effort to control and minimize her effects.

Goldman felt we would die if we could not dream about what could lie ahead of us. She was sure that if people did not dream of a future where equality and tolerance exist, it would never come to pass. And if we don't dream of better, why do we continue our pursuit of the truth?

Where will we find a path forward if these concepts are not perpetuated for everyone? How will we discover what is just for all of us, and how can a community you live in decide what is fair for you?

Emma Goldman wrote, "if voting changes anything, they will make it illegal." Having voting available to all citizens would be an admirable goal. It would make our society more inclusive!

So, here we are left with a dilemma of excluding residents of our nation from voting and having a voice. The problem is perhaps that we shouldn't be upset because we let this happen. If there was another option and that road was never considered, isn't it time to open another route and see if that one works?

Remember, if that one choice doesn't work, we can keep thinking and providing additional choices because we know that we are at another intersection; we can make other choices or find other options. That, too, fails to stop the bleeding. We will know we must think again and offer more choices to survive. However, we still must continue to talk!

We could be up to the task ahead, and new choices could promote better answers! Our current path has outlived its usefulness. The people who started this path are no longer with us. Perhaps we need a new direction for the next generations.

We require strong motivation from people who will advance our choices so that we can pursue a better path ahead for all of us. The road we have started on is fraught with negatives and unanswered questions. Thinking about these negatives and unanswered questions brings up the concept that thinking is imperative, and you cannot avoid thinking about other options and choices without risking stagnation.

Just because there exists a pattern of racism in our community ingrained in law and the minds of all Americans regarding slavery, segregation, ghettos, Jim Crow laws, Black Lives Matter, etc., doesn't mean that we can't change.

The words in the Preamble to our Constitution meant equality in the 18th century. How does that compare to the definition of equality today? In fact, what kind of equality can we count on in the 21st century?

People of color have learned to deal with the vast amount of respect still being denied. These Black American citizens, residents in America and ours, deserve respect and rights, despite the cloud over their heads for centuries, as they protest for their unalienable rights. Pigpen, a character in the *Peanuts* comic strip drawn by Charles Schulz, was different from the other kids. Only Charlie Brown unconditionally accepted Pigpen for who he was, even defending and accepting him for his differences. We all must find how our paths lead to a common path of inclusion, and we must be resolute about it.

We live free; we savor what being free means now, and we seriously must sit down and discuss what *Free, Liberty, an﹒ Equality* will mean for our children, grandchildren, great-grandchildren, and this country. Based on what has transpired in our life leads me to

believe that our work has only just begun.

Let's return to the thought of education. A movement in America calls for an updated history curriculum – the truth about history. We must stop only presenting the White hero and show the aftermath of how those views impacted Blacks and women.

The new curriculum must list the full story: the good and the bad. Diversity of thought and opinion is valued, essential, and integral to our ideals!

Diversity of thought and opinion is valued as an integral part of every one of these decisions. That's too bad. Our forebears were never considered perfect. Indeed, we are not perfect today. No humans are! But once we start to produce discussions that can end with majorities agreeing with each other on the basis that all can understand, these meetings can correct the direction we are traveling. We can find a path we can all seek and attain rational progress.

Do people need to consider the opinions of others? Talk about what people say and offer other alternatives and choices. Perhaps people can just agree that some perspectives will produce opinions and attract a majority; I didn't know the case should make those opinions, even if something they're wrong, lead us on the wrong track. That should be the model.

How can that be considered wrong when it comes time to vote to approve the plans after they were debated and discussed? It was apparent that there might be portions that were not dealt with. Still, in the end, even some of those opinions might even be discarded might provide Future Hope for consensus. Everyone appeals to everyone's opinion needing to be valued.

George Orwell, in his novel *1984*, said, "whoever controls the past controls the future" (Orwell, 1949). If we start with that truth, often we can survive in knowing the past. So let us retrace the steps that we have taken.

Critical Race Theory (CRT) is a body of legal scholarship and an academic movement in United States history, but it is not limited to just that. Civil rights scholars determine the facts about the conflicts witnessed throughout the last 200 years; at its core, it deals with the struggle between races and the concepts of liberty and freedom but is primarily concerned with the freedom of expression.

These two concepts, liberty and freedom, make up the essence of what people consider to be the precepts of sociology and culture. Anthropologists believe many aspects of sociology in their work as well. Culture and community do not depend on class or color. Socialization through groups and columns and common patterns use living relationships as necessary to create a culture by which socialization is spread through interaction among various cultures.

In this way, the quality of life improves and expands by including others who live alongside you so that different plans can blend in as experiences are shared with other groups. Cultural practices, mores, and folkways blend by intermingling these social patterns.

Sometimes there are intermarriages, and over time, a sharing of new family patterns along with education, compassion, love, and the concept of tolerance occurs. The idea of truth holds all of these interactions together with significance for many people. Once trust emerges from these relationship interactions, this trust can lead to the creation of new cultural patterns.

We must find others to help move the needle to that next step. You can see that path with new opinions and ideas, but you must come with compassion so others can find the moral courage to hold on to what you are constructing to communicate, smile, and laugh.

Conversation and the blending of opinions can do much over time to make the process easier. However, you need to take chances, smile, and extend yourself. You must consider socializing and laughing with people stressing similarities, not differences.

This wasn't a cultural thing or a racial thing; it was primarily a thought process. Most enslaved Black people were freed in 1863 by President Abraham Lincoln through the Emancipation Proclamation. Despite this freedom, there was a lot of pain, heartache, terror, lack of education, and attitudes that must all be shifted for the new law to be applied to actions and behaviors. But it takes a generation of positive thinking to change the country's mindset.

Blacks were at a loss about how to act as free persons. Add to that fact that White people did not know how to live with their freed property. These thoughts permeated the thinking of the White enslavers. They had to consider what the word free meant. Then they had to think, what do free men do? Do they get to make decisions for themselves? Where do I have to be?

So, now I am a free man; what is it that I am supposed to do? Many Southern Black men had to deal with the answer to that question. Nobody saw this question coming, but now these formerly enslaved people are surrounded by thousands of Southerners who were now hostile to their former property, who are now supposed to be free. They had to deal with questions that nobody ever considered what do free men do?

Do they get to decide for themselves? These Blacks had no idea how the word freed applied to them. Here are the questions:

Where do I have to be?
When do I have to do that?
Why must it be my question?
How do I answer these questions?
How do I decide for myself what needs to be done or said?

Southern Blacks faced the unforeseen experience of being freemen, but they also had to consider if they were still surrounded by thousands of Southerners who were not hostile to them. But they were the former property of these men who were they supposed to be free from. Blacks were at a loss about how to act as free people. Add to the fact that Whites did not know how to live with their free freed property.

Southern Blacks thought about their situation, which had just been sprung upon them. Most had not been educated; most didn't yet did not even know what school was and what was supposed to be taught in that school.

The Reconstruction Era lasted from 1866 to 1877, and its job was to provide the paths that each seceded state would have to take to rejoin the union that they had left by their own choice. Southern enslavers maintained some bitterness as they again tried to belong to the union. They had few options.

Northerners teemed into Dixie. Teachers attempted to address all of the questions that were asked about southern schools and all of the students who needed their help. The newly freed Blacks did not know how to blend in, and the Whites had never considered involving Black children in their schools. The question of orientation to get these Black students into schools was never discussed; options were never even considered. What were they supposed to do?

Those questions had to be answered by the White former slaveholders doing what formerly was acceptable practice, and education did not solve all the problems across the question of the newly freed Black slaves were not considered.

New thinking was going on. The minds of everyone, Black and White, male and female, and adults, all had new roles. Freedom and liberty require learning skills. Whites and Blacks started doing things they never thought about. These people had to accept new responsibilities. Many people had to accept new roles.

All of this was not easy. Then they had to consider what work needed to be performed now that there were no enslaved people.

Who would be called on to make sure that the work was completed?

There were more than four million stories about this area as the Black population grew. During the years preceding the shots at Fort Sumter, it is said that just 25,000 White Americans owned over 500,000 enslaved people in South Carolina. Black women and Black men were forced to marry and have their children raised as a new generation of enslaved people.

In the years between the Constitutional Convention in 1787 and the Banning of the slave trade in 1808, it is believed that the landowners in those states bought more than 100,000 new enslaved Black people. But, despite these horrible stories that must be retold and remembered, there is a ton of healing applied for getting all of the things that have happened for centuries, thoughts held by Blacks and Whites overlapped. Still, they did not have the console themselves about the path ahead.

You must find others to help move the needle to that next step. You can see that path with new opinions and ideas, but you must come with compassion so others can find the moral courage to hold on to what you are constructing to communicate, smile, and laugh.

Conversation and the blending of opinions can do much over time to make the process easier. However, you need to take chances, smile, and extend yourself. You must consider socializing and laughing with people stressing similarities, not differences.

America, we can do this. Let us sit down and listen to one another. Let's discuss complex past events and find a way to discuss what we've learned together.

Now, instead of blaming one group and victimizing another, let's accept the truth as it was and step forward together, creating the *present* that will give a history unlike any other found on earth

—one of living together, working together, and being peaceful together.

17

Truman A Quiet Example

"No one who ever gave his/ her best regretted it."
– George Halas

"Come on, Jeff! Hurry up, or you'll miss it," my sister said. I darted after her and my parents through a small crowd gathering along the streets of Miami, Florida. My seven-year-old legs were pumped with excitement, and I arrived at the corner of two streets with my family, where I stood waiting with everyone else.

"Do you think he'll notice me?" I asked my mom?

"I hope so, I hope so!" she said.

I remember looking at all the people on the sidewalks. Some held signs; others were waving little banners and flags. We were all waiting and stepping from side to side, some were still, and others were looking up and down the streets. I did the same thing. It helped to pass the time.

I heard the sirens of the motorcade. Suddenly the crowd started clapping and cheering. I could only see the crowd, but I knew he was coming.

"Just think!" I said to my sister, "President Truman, here!" My sister squealed and turned back to face the street.

The clapping started and rolled down the street like an ocean wave. My feet started tingling, and I could feel it race up and land in my belly—the noise, the clapping, the cheering.

Suddenly I saw him! President Truman was standing in the open car within the motorcade! The sunlight bounced off the polished bumpers like a beacon of light as it rolled toward the corner where we stood.

The car slowed down and came to a stop—in front of me. In his light-colored suit, Harry S. Truman stood and waved at everyone on the street. He was looking right at me. He reached over and patted me on the head. His hand slid from my head to my cheek. I felt an electric current race through my head and down to my tingling toes! My tingling stomach turned into a hurricane of butterflies.

He said, "If you are ever in Washington, stop by the White House. That's where I live!" I answered loudly, "yes, sir," as my head bobbed up and down, nodding.

Truman dropped his hand and looked at my family. I swear he gave us a wink! President Truman then turned to the rest of the crowd, waved, moved away from the window, and the driver slowly turned the corner and drove away from us.

I looked at my mom; she was dabbing her eyes, and my sister's mouth was still open in a comical o-shape. With a grin, ear to ear, I shook my head and was speechless.

I had met the President of the United States, Harry S. Truman. He had patted my head and touched my cheek. I burned that day into my memory forever.

Why do I share this story of my life with you? Because people impact other people. People's ideas, work, and agendas can affect how you experience this life. Many things are out of our control, and so we have to roll with it for a while, but that doesn't mean we have to live with things that way forever.

We can be the influencers and make the changes we want to see, which is what I want to share with you. President Harry S. Truman influenced my life in those brief few minutes, but he also influenced millions in a quiet and humbling way.

President Truman was born on May 8, 1884, in the town of Lamar, Missouri. Truman grew up in Independence, only ten miles east of Kansas City. As a child, he worked on the family farm, devoured books, played the piano, and wanted to be a great soldier. He desired to go to West Point but was not eligible to attend because of his poor eyesight. He did not have enough money to attend a four-year college, so he joined the National Guard.

He fell in love with Virginia, "Bess" Wallace, and asked her to marry him, but she refused. But, he never gave up on her. He joined a friend as he started a mining business, but Truman did not stay very long as the company did not take off.

Eventually, his unit was called up, and he was shipped to France as part of the American Expeditionary Force fighting the World War. The soldiering life suited Truman. However, his unit was known for unruliness and ineffectiveness, but Truman helped turn it into a top-notch unit.

Truman returned from the war and became a haberdasher. He married Bess in 1919 and five years later had their first and only child, Mary Margaret. His haberdashery business eventually failed, but in 1922, Thomas J. Pendergast, the Democratic boss of Kansas City, asked Truman to run for a judgeship on the county court of Jackson County's eastern district.

Truman served one term, was defeated for a second, and then became a presiding judge in 1926, a position he held until 1934. As presiding judge, Truman managed the county's finances during the early years of the Great Depression and established a reputation for personal integrity, honesty, and efficiency.

In 1934, Truman was elected to the U.S. Senate and gained national attention during World War II when he chaired the "Truman Committee." It investigated government defense spending. With that notice, President Franklin D. Roosevelt chose Truman as his running mate in the 1944 presidential campaign.

According to research, FDR needed Truman largely because the "Missourian passed muster with Southern Democrats and party officials." They won, and after only eighty-two days as Vice President, with the death of FDR on April 12, 1945, Harry S. Truman became the thirty-third President of the United States. Truman was far more bookish than many of the nation's better-educated leaders. His application of history to modern circumstances and issues set Truman apart from other Presidents. He learned from past mistakes to fashion a better today and tomorrow for the country.

Now the challenging work began. World War II had been raging for years, and the European theater was about to end. However, fighting in the Pacific theater looked long and drawn out. Truman was told about the 200,000 soldiers it would take to invade Japan, and the number of causalities they predicted was sickening. He did not have the heart for it.

He was also informed about the success of the Manhattan Project. This option would save hundreds of thousands of American lives, but what would be the cost to Japan? The morality of the Manhattan Project and the A-bomb question ran deep, but Truman approved of its use against Japan. On August 6 and 9, 1945, the U.S. Army Air Force dropped atomic bombs on two cities, Hiroshima and Nagasaki.

Following the close of World War II, he knew that a new plan had to be implemented. War needed to end, and peace needed to prevail once again. Truman's presidency coincided with the golden age of statecraft when the U.S. embedded its unrivaled power in foreign affairs, and this laid the foundation for what we do today: The UN, NATO, Four Point Plan, The Truman Doctrine, the Marshall Plan, and the Shuman Plan.

Truman was responsible for putting forth the United Nations. The United Nations (UN) is an international organization committed to maintaining international peace and security, developing friendly relations among nations, and promoting social progress, better living standards, and human rights. In the years after World War II, Truman worked diligently to ensure that the United Nations—conceived by President Franklin D. Roosevelt was a forum in which differences between nations could be resolved before they led to war. It would be a significant player in international life by committing fifty-one countries to maintain international peace and security, living standards, and human rights.

Next came the North Atlantic Treaty Organization - NATO. NATO is a collective defense to help stop aggression from other countries from reaching destructive levels in the European theater. Truman said NATO "would create a shield against aggression and fear of aggression--a bulwark which would permit us to get on with the real business of . . . achieving a fuller and happier life for all of our citizens."

Truman added, "By this treaty, we are not only seeking to establish freedom from aggression and the use of force in the North Atlantic Community, but we are also actively striving to promote and preserve peace worldwide."

The Truman Doctrine was for the betterment of people and demonstrated that the United States would not return to isolationism after World War II. The U.S. would take an active role in world affairs. Truman oversaw efforts like the famous *Berlin Airlift.* It was an operation that carried food, fuel, and other supplies into West Berlin by plane but also kept the American and Soviet soldiers from confronting each other and beginning an explosive battle. The effort required careful planning and resources, but the Airlift allowed the United States to keep a foothold in post-war Germany. To further help rebuild after the war, the United States pledged $13 billion of aid to Europe in the form of the Marshall Plan (ERP).

All of this was happening because the Soviet Union was not backing down from its invasion of many Eastern European countries. The Soviet Union no longer wanted to extend the fighting but did not want to leave their current invaded positions. The Truman Doctrine's full purpose was to give aid to countries suffering from the aftermath of World War II and still threatened by Soviet oppression.

Unfortunately, The Cold War's foundation had been laid by what the Soviet Union was doing, but Truman did his best to confront Soviet aggression without triggering World War III. He fought back with aid to the oppressed people and keep NATO and the U.N. strengthened.

The Korean War globalized the Cold War and spurred a massive American military build-up that began the nuclear arms race. The President used the rules of the U.N. to help defend South Korea. Unfortunately, the conflict settled into a bloody and grisly stalemate that would not be resolved until Truman left office in 1953.

Next came point Four. It was announced in 1950 and was technical assistance that involved sending experts into the field to teach skills and to help solve problems in their areas of specialization, such as irrigation, agriculture, fisheries, education, public health, or forestry in European nations.

Truman was also involved in the Schumann plan; Truman supported the plan to help steel mills rebuild in Europe. It proposed the creation of a European Coal and Steel Community, whose members would pool coal and steel production again to help Europe become independent and self-sufficient.

Truman reorganized the United States military and national security. He needed a way to communicate better, and the National Security Act was passed in 1947. The legislation had three main purposes.

1. It unified the Army, Navy, and Air Force under a National Military.
2. Establishment (NME) headed by a civilian Secretary of Defense. It was later renamed the Department of Defense.

3. The National Security Act also created the Central Intelligence Agency (CIA), the leading arm of the nation's intelligence network.

4. Finally, the Act established the National Security Council (NSC) to advise the President on issues related primarily to American foreign policy.

On the home front, Truman had other battles. These battles would lay the foundation for the Civil Rights movement of the 1960s. I'm sure you've heard a little bit about that.

Truman's first battle was the desegregation of the U.S. military. On July 26, 1948, Truman signed Executive Order 9981, creating the President's Committee on Equality of Treatment and Opportunity in the Armed Services.

> The order stated:
>
> It is hereby declared to be the policy of the President [and the United States] that there shall be equality of treatment and opportunity for all persons in the armed services without regard to *race, color, religion, or national origin.* This policy shall be implemented as rapidly as possible due to the time required to effectuate any necessary changes without impairing efficiency or morale.

This was a great start, but it would take generations to help people's mindsets change.

Like many Civil Rights challenges, the pushback of change and tradition usually happened, but it took time. Truman received pushback from politicians, generals, and friends, who opposed an integrated military. Truman wrote in response to his detractors, "I am asking for equal opportunity for all human beings, and as long as I stay here, I am going to continue that fight." I hope you can see why I like him and include him in this important book.

The Air Force supported President Turman and was the first fully integrated military branch. But, in the South, the Jim Crow Laws were in full force. The freedom that needed to come would not happen until twenty years later. Isn't that typically what happens here in America? We have one set of laws, but then there is a gap in how we apply them. What hubris!

Truman's support of civil rights surprised many people because of his upbringing. Remember how Truman grew up in a former slave state where his small-town, rural surroundings included segregation and subordination for many of its citizens? What was shocking about this was that even within his ancestry, there were slaveholders.

Well before Truman became the President, he saw, as a judge, firsthand the plight of Black Americans in urban areas and was sympathetic to their cause.

Unfortunately, after being a judge and becoming President, Truman saw how Black Americans and Black veterans returning from World War II were poorly treated at home. Truman heard reports from his advisors about how Black soldiers, who had just returned from overseas, were being dumped out of Army trucks in Mississippi and beaten.

Truman was recorded as saying following this incident, "Whatever my inclinations as a native of Missouri might have been, as President, I know this is bad. I shall fight to end evils like this."

According to a report in the Truman Library, other episodes of violence profoundly moved Truman. In 1946, a mob shot and killed two Black men and their wives in Georgia. No one ever stood trial for the crime. And, in South Carolina, police pulled Army Sergeant Isaac Woodard from a bus and beat him with nightsticks, permanently blinding him.

Why? Black Americans had every right to expect justice under the American system, but what happened in this case? Do you remember chapter 2—you have to be taught how to hate?

These events left a deep impression on the President in a way that no statistics ever could. In late 1946, Harry Truman established "The President's Committee on Civil Rights." President Truman said the following to its members. "I want our Bill of Rights implemented! We have been trying to do this for 150 years. We're making progress, but we're not making progress fast enough."

Truman's fight for Civil Rights was a tough battle. This was 1948, over 80 years since the Civil War, yet this battle was still happening! He asked Congress to support a Civil Rights package that included "federal protection against lynching, better protection of the right to vote, and a permanent Fair Employment Practices Commission."

Truman's proposal with Congress met strong opposition and led to the splintering of the Democratic Party right before the 1948 presidential election. Truman won reelection, but little Civil Rights legislation was enacted during his administration.

In 1948, according to a speech Truman made in Sedalia, Missouri, he said, "I believe in the brotherhood of man, not merely the brotherhood of White men, but the *brotherhoo* of all men before the law. I believe in the Constitution and the Declaration of Independence. In giving the [Blacks] the rights which are theirs, we are only acting in accord with our ideals of a true democracy."

Truman later wrote, "Discrimination is a disease; we must attack it wherever it appears."

How would the foundation for Civil Rights have been laid without President Truman? Without Truman, how would the armed forces have been desegregated? Without Truman, how would the awareness of humanity, peace, and fairness have been brought into discussion and action?

President Truman was a crafty fellow, who used his native self-confidence and leadership ability, applied his old-fashioned American horse sense, and took the situation he was given (by the death of Roosevelt) and improved it to better the circumstances and experiences of others. He believed that all who had fought for freedom had fought for the *free•om an• brotherhoo• of all people,* and he laid the foundation for a movement that he would see power-fully expressed in the philosophical future of America. Even though he was no longer the President, he lived to see the early effects of the Civil Rights Act.

To sum it all up, the decisive and thoughtful Harry S. Truman put the icing on the cake when he not only led us to successful conclusions of the Second World War and the Korean War, but America became the predominant nation on Earth. Truman had a placard on his desk until he left the White House. In his quiet and humbling way, the words on the placard said, "The Buck Stops Here." It rang true without him saying a word. His actions are a testimony to the character of our thirty-third President.

18

The Second Convention

"You can't go back and change the beginning, but you can start where you are and
change the ending."– Unknown.

The title of this book is called *Secon♦ Chances.* We have come to
the chapter that is my most comprehensive proposal yet! It is that
way for a profound reason.

We consider our Constitution's opening words in our preamble: *We, the People.* There has been no indication from our story
and its gathering of evidence that anybody or group of people in
any state gave any direction or hints that would provide a path
forward. We just read these words, do not think about their
significance, and don't apply them to anything. They remain as
words. No one has ever applied these words to the living forms
found in our country.

In 1786, the first gathering of the Constitutional Convention met in Annapolis, Maryland, but they quickly departed because only five states sent parts of a delegation. No one knew about it, but this was the idea, and it was part of a secret. When so few people were involved in the process, the convention could not go on, hardly representing enough of the people to make the proceedings official.

We cannot be justified when so few people are involved in the process. Less than 2% of the residents of our country ever knew anything about the 1787 Convention held in Carpenters Hall in Philadelphia. Most people were never informed about the convention; it was a secret. It kept most of the people out of the convention's discussions and the new government's creation.

In short, the discussions were not publicized or reported, and I feel they were not even discussed adequately inside Carpenters Hall. Nothing about it was discussed. Few people outside of the debates themselves offered ideas to be considered.

This entire event in Philadelphia could be considered a travesty. It might even be considered an oligarchy of the wealthy and propertied classes who attended that convention. It certainly wasn't a democratic plan. But, that exercise in democracy was only an exercise, and what they produced was not even supported by all participants who attended. As you have read and seen the evidence throughout the book, they tried to make life easier for wealthy landowners and slaveholders. Clearly, not all of the participating delegations were there for that.

Surprisingly, to this writer, one of those who voted "no" in 1787 was later elected to the office of Vice President of the United States - Elbridge Gerry.

Our story has not provided any new facts. Perhaps so few of us have even considered those events of 1787 today, but now, the questions remain unanswered because many don't care. Aren't there enough people who think we might take up this issue again to see if we can solve the dilemma that all of these events have left us with? This could be our *Secon⸱ Chance.*

This author *⸱oes* care. That is why I am suggesting our *Secon⸱ Chance* to begin a national conversation to initiate the process of reconsidering how our Constitution serves ALL our needs, inclusive of ALL our citizens. I propose that we hold another Constitutional Convention and, this time, for the first time, have the entire country participate! Let's look at everything as an absolute majority and discuss, share ideas, and help to change things so that we all have a *Secon⸱ Chance!*

People could make suggestions. We could start a dialogue. Perhaps, with more people participating, thousands of others will listen, think, and experience, and maybe what they speak about might improve what we currently have before us.

That dialogue needs to be expanded to include more people. As we go forward, I will suggest several significant steps, but we all must agree to find our real truths, believe them, and follow where those truths lead us to our most essential values.

We must enforce constitutional limitations. We must advance the concept of the right of all citizens to vote. All citizens must be allowed to participate in our elections. Their judgments must be allowed to speak, compete, and be considered so that anybody can follow those arguments, evaluate them, and put them before the majority of us; all of us must be allowed to win the day and participate, but it won't happen if we don't intentionally make room for it to happen!

But *why* is this a necessity?

Truth has to prevail because only the truth can promote intrinsic value. But our Framers believed that separation of powers and checks and balances would provide the *balance wheel* so that truth would prevail and provide inherent value that would promote Liberty, protect freedoms and perpetuate our way of life. But we must always consider all minorities!

As you have read in chapter after chapter, the problem with America's Constitution was that only a select few made the decisions for the majority. They were in it for themselves and not thinking about future generations.

We, together, cannot always be wrong. If those in Congress genuinely represent their constituency and perform their duties according to what their constituency wants, then the government would truly represent the people. But that doesn't happen enough of the time. Lobbyists and special interest groups funded by corporate interests and the economic elite (the minority) demand what is in their best interest, forcing and enforcing that on every citizen (the majority). This is not fair.

Now, the way the Constitution currently exists, the choices left to us can work if those in power (legislative and executive) represent the majority of us. If they don't do that, we are left to inherit their garbage for the next generation.

Isn't this the basis of tyranny?

The power of John Locke's logic and the thought of Montesquieu need to be a part of the equation to foster changes and meaningful growth that benefit subsequent generations.

Americans were and are divided in many ways. Listen to the evening news, and you see how we are still not one whole nation today because some of the population continues to fall victim to the rest. Yes, we have had Amendments to the Constitution—the 13th, 14th, 15th, and 19th that finally started the pathway to equality, but why couldn't it have started equally for all in the first place and much earlier than it did?

What if we, as a majority, sat down together and kept the simple focus of the word equality? What if the men in that room in 1787 would have agreed to free the slaves, allowing Blacks and women to vote, and encompassed an education to give each person, regardless of race, sex, creed, and color, the same opportunities from the start? I believe that so many lives would have been empowered.

What if we sat down and we talked about shared views, shared interests, and the profound value of equality?

The history that most people are taught shows that the Founders tried to become one nation, which looked good on paper. (Well, don't most plans on paper look excellent until you add the key ingredient—people!)

What if the Founders would have recognized that only one thing, that we are all of us human! We are only one race—the same team—the human race. That would have leveled the playing field, and our history would not be riddled with flaws. However, in the same breath, I must admit that we are only human—bound to make mistakes, are flawed, and are prideful.

America, we are all one human race. And yet, we are still split because of race, religion, gender, and color. We should be better.

Out of necessity, we should be better. In fact, you have to believe it can be better.

The message has been sent and received many times, but the thoughts in that message have not been heard, nor have they been remembered for quite a while. For each generation, it has to be repeated again and again. That's too bad. *We have to be carefully taught;* our goals must be cohesive. And this time, together, we have to repeat and restate our goal.

America needs to make our *Second Chance* work, and together we must look at our values to restate those goals and move forward.

America has to ensure the success of our *Second Chance.* We have to make our vital choices succeed and not drop the ball! America has to ensure success, but it will require all of us to get behind it.

Many people have tried to get us back on track and failed because people were not paying attention or ready for change. We must try again.

Let's see if another attempt catches on and if America can listen to each other this time. Previous generations only heard parts of that message. Because of the limitations of time and methods of communication, they decided to listen to themselves and not anyone else because that was all they heard.

Where are the long-lasting benefits of checks and balances supposed to come from if the government is run by political parties/forces that change every few years? Who thinks about their share of the pie and doesn't want to share it?

It's still federalist even though we are in the 21st century and we wear different clothing and there are different parties, but they misconstrue what's going on, and one of them takes control, and changes are considered.

We need people to recruit people. We need informed elected representatives who believe in inclusive values to lead us—not just lobbyists and special interest groups funded by corporate interests and the economic elite who fund and manipulate political power for their benefit.

If it doesn't come to pass, our representatives are no better than the elite 55 White men who ignored the majority and met secretly in 1787.

Remember that public office is not an entitlement - it must be earned. Legislators must remember that they represent the people's needs and not just their wants. They are not entitled just because of their office. A public office is a public trust. Why doesn't that thought resonate today?

The Constitution granted freedom of speech does not protect U.S. citizens from the proliferation of lies and baseless claims that seek to manipulate the 'news' and how our land is governed. Those in power must stop pushing their agenda to blindside the American people. And we, as a country, need to ask what is in everyone's best interest and not only 'what's in it for me?'

Where is the truth to come from in the public square? We hear versions of that truth from newspapers, magazines, and television. People who get their ideas out are to be applauded for their interest in addressing the day's issues, but they can't make decisions for anyone.

Now, this is what I want to say about what's currently going on. These are my thoughts about our Constitution and what I have been thinking about for a long time. Your thoughts are welcome as additions, *pro or con,* and need to be offered as long as we're all in the public square.

I sincerely believe that any changes offered must start with the preamble. If the goals of our Constitutional Convention began with this part of the Constitution, I think that is so because so few of these goals have been achieved. It has been 246 years. I think it's time.

This author believes that these ideals we admire have declined in value because they have been stagnant for these 246 years and that none of them have ever approached becoming the bedrock of America!

We have not ensured that words affect the people of our land and improve their lives. We can forget about *securing* anything for our posterity because we cannot pretend any longer than any of these ideals have been addressed ever since 1787.

Have we established justice for all of us? Do we have any semblance of domestic tranquility? We might have made some strides toward promoting the general welfare, but they are not consistent, have not been expressed regularly, and have they ever been applied to all of us? Do these goals help make this nation better?

We certainly have not secured the blessings of liberty for ourselves or our children, so how can we have made any strides forward for our posterity?

The Constitution of the United States under which we live has been here all these years, but no part of that document has provided a path toward achieving those goals!

It took England from 1215 to 1625 and then to 1689 to get where they were able to find a way to perpetuate what they had built and maintained for even some of their people. We followed their lead in several ways, one of which was to perpetuate the capacity that we could do it ourselves.

I advocate for us to take our Second Chance! We know what we have, but I think we need a clarion to get us a road to follow so that we can get to work.

We have the strength to do this! However, we must find the will to do it! We must provide a signpost to show us the way and welcome others to participate with us. Don't waste time. Each of these people who want to participate has to demonstrate that they have the courage and the will to move forward, so we do not waste any more time. We must provide signposts to show us how and welcome others to participate.

In 1927, in the case of Grain versus Doherty, the Supreme Court affirmed the power of inquiry. It provided a means to enforce the results of that inquiry through the legislative function as a part of Congress which possessed oversight authority. This was considered part of the concept of checks and balances and felt like an essential part of advice and consent.

I will share my opinions on Amendments 1 through 10. When they were written in the 18th century, they were necessary at the time. However, many of these provide parts that no longer pertain to the realities of the 21st Century. They were not relevant to the times of the 19th or 20th centuries, and they certainly do not provide a path forward for us.

How are these provisions to be enforced for each generation? How can we live with the changes of the past and apply them to the present day and the future? The only way that can be done is through education.

Our first amendment details rights to freedom of religion and practicing it, but these precepts are disobeyed daily. No prosecutions have followed. Freedom of speech is frequently prevented so that a redress of grievances is never pursued because our citizens might believe that no one will listen or think people don't care.

Despite Thomas Jefferson's warning, "Avenues used for the truth must ALWAYS BE MAINTAINED." Jefferson himself did not respect his warning. That has not been the practice in this country. It's been largely ignored from the beginning.

Our Second Amendment needs to be maintained, and the number of guns available to our citizens must be limited to protect those without guns.

Those who carry weapons illegally and kill innocent people must be dealt with. We shouldn't excuse insurrections and murders of *innocent* believers in a cause. This needs to be addressed by restricting entitlement to carry a loaded weapon in a public realm.

Our third amendment is outdated. No one should be forced to provide sanctuary for our Armed Forces; that's why we have military bases, a selective service system, and State militias.

Amendments that follow, such as the fourth, fifth, and sixth amendments, which protect liberty and justice, should never be restricted. Still, they could be re-stated elsewhere, rephrased, and included in the content of the new document.

The seventh Amendment needs to be maintained but could be re-examined. How relevant is the issue with common law? Couldn't these issues be considered under *Consi*erations for Future Legislation?

However, *trial by jury* must remain part of the bedrock of America's story. Our peers must be part of that regardless of race, creed, sex, or national origin, trial by jury again must remain part of the bedrock of America's story. It must not be touched!

The eighth amendment should be retained, as should the ninth and tenth amendments.

Article 1 could be tightened somewhat by abetting census-takers, maintaining registration records, and rechecking the counting of the poor and some rule citizens or minority groups who might resist being counted because of their immigrant status or because of cultural prejudices.

White census-takers might deny Black Americans and their totals because of the skin color of those citizens and prisoners in prison. Their votes aren't taken because they made a mistake and are denied their vote because they made that mistake. All should be entire to a *Secon▸ Chance.*

Intellectual property rights need to be reconsidered. Why should their creation not be protected? The trolling and stealing of their intellectual creations. Perhaps we should prepare for increases in our population and, over the years, reallocate voting rules. We need more representatives.

Executives' private holdings have to come under formal scrutiny so as not to confound the seeking of the truth. They always try to claim it was not their intention. We have to allow for some detective work to allow appointed people to find the sources of income who earn money in this county or who live outside of the country. If laws are broken, *no one is exempt from prosecution.*

Article 2: Bribery or treason rules to be established for those misdeeds while in office. Rules will identify the processes that should be added and enforced.

The popular vote news is to be considered. Electoral votes should not count (look up the electoral college and why it is unfair). Voting for the people is so important. We can't subject ourselves to the electoral college. These additions must be considered in the second constitutional process's second drafting.

We need to start this possibility. Boy scouts say, *be prepare*. It is not too early to have our second constitutional convention. Time passes, and it could be late for change.

The ninth amendment needs to be reconsidered. I suggest adding these words: "maintaining different standards toward difference citizens depending on their color, sexual orientation, or beliefs." Why shouldn't we consider adding these thoughts, disparaging others' beliefs about what we believe, and expanding our citizenship?

Why don't each of us participate? Think about it and add your opinion and discuss your ideas with others. You and I have the right to elucidate your thoughts contribute to the process and have your voice heard.

Article 3: Term limits need to be reconsidered. I propose for the Judicial Branch a time frame of 20 years. That's a generation. That should be enough. That is what our first Congress thought and what Thomas Jefferson thought.

The nominations to our Supreme Court should be limited in the number of appointments to be made. We must be more open to people who don't look like us, even in selecting candidates for Congress or the Supreme Court.

Have we expanded the size of our Congress, Senate, or Court? We are now more than 300 million citizens. We have devalued this because of our delays. We need to expand the court to accommodate the responsibility of our expanding citizenry, which will be 400 million citizens before you know it.

If you have thoughts about this progress, you should express them. Your participation is as meaningful as mine. Everyone should discuss issues, provisions, and alternatives and find a way to participate in our democracy. We all desire and deserves a voice. ISN'T IT TIME?

Stephan Breyer was born August 125, 1938, in San Francisco; he graduated from Stanford in 1959 and Harvard Law school in 1964. After more than twenty years as a Supreme Court Justice, Breyer has always been lauded for his pragmatic approach to the law. He has worked with all factions of both major political parties.

Breyer has always considered the consequences of his choices. He remained a thinker, weighing options and outcomes.

When judicial appointees have present opinions, many follow those choices, but many adhere to the past, and rather than consider what could be, they wind up preferring what is. They fail to consider what could be and accept what is correct.

That is to say that many follow precedents and adhere to the past and its history. However, this concept of stare decisis (the legal principle of determining points in litigation according to precedent) cannot be ignored, which limits the path forward and the considerations of other points of view.

In the world that we live in 2022, the unwillingness to reconsider the past and weigh the value of other pertinent options which might someday prevail and provide new truths cannot help less than some of those found on the road we have traveled in our history.

When we include more of us in the process of change and more voices and opinions in search of the truth, we can only make the future a brighter place.

Legal standards can be reconsidered as time goes on and include others who might come to the fore to encourage us to think about how we can become a more equal nation for all of us.

With these words, I wish to place in nomination the name of Stephan G. Breyer as my first choice for President of America's Second Constitutional Convention.

19

Summary

"Don't cry over the past, it's gone.
Don't stress over the future, it hasn't arrived.
Live in the present.
Do what you can.
Don't stop - make it beautiful.
Be proud. You helped bring change about."
–Anonymous

Dear Reader,

As your teacher, I thank you for taking the time to read this book. Since you were my students, my goal was to tell you the whole story of how our country came to be. I know I could not include every story, but I wanted to share the untold stories, and with those, you have the truth.

The philosopher Socrates argued that absolute Truth is knowable and that we communicate best when we communicate only that Truth. I have presented truths here, and I feel that you have been my student through this process.

Socrates' student, Plato, took the truth a step further, saying that "one can arrive at the Truth" through dialectic—which meant a process of questioning and testing. Plato believed that there are truths to be discovered; that knowledge is possible. Moreover, he held that truth is not, as the Sophists thought, relative. Instead, it is objective; it is that which our reason, used rightly, apprehends.

Plato also said, "The mind creates reality. We can change our reality by changing our mind." What is your mind telling you? How can the words on this page impact you so that you want to give this country a *Secon♦ Chance*?

Now that you have everything, will you do me a favor? Will you look at how the pendulum is swinging in society? If it goes too far to the right or the left, we will continue to have problems. Please study both sides of the argument and remember to ask yourself the most crucial question: *why?* Think, ponder, question, research, and remember that all should have a voice at the table. All should be woven into the fabric of America. You know from the truth of this book what happens when it is neglected.

I started this project in 1967. My thoughts have been about you, this country, and this book for over 50 years of my adult life. I have researched, taught, expanded, pondered, written, and rewritten this book more than I can recall. And now, in 2022, it is time to give everyone a *Secon♦ Chance* at the truth you deserve.

Thank you for not giving up and persevering to the end. You and your children now have the *Secon♦ Chance* they were looking for. Be well, and as a final reminder, always ask the question, *why?*

Yours Sincerely,
Jeffrey Ellner

Notes

Chapter 1

U.S. Const. Publ. https://www.archives.gov/founding-docs/constitution-transcript

U.S. Bill of Rights. U.S. Const. amend. I–X.

Chapter 2

Hammerstein, Oscar. Rodgers, Richard. "You've Got to be Carefully Taught," *South Pacific,* 1949.

Ebenstein, William. *Great Political Thinkers.* Rinehart & Company. 1951.

Chapter 3

Atwood, Roger. "City Politics," Archaeology. May 2019. https://rogeratwood.com/?s=city+politics

Beals, Ralph, & Hijer, Harry. *An Introuction to Anthropology.* The Macmillan Company. 1959.

Berreman, Gerald et al. *Anthropology Toay.* CRM Bools. 1971

Chang, Kenneth. Shards of Space Rock That Killed Dinosaurs May Have Been Found at Fossil Site," New York Times. April 8, 2022.

Minister, Christopher. "Ten Facts About the Ancient Olmecs," April 16, 2018.

Swartz, Marc. *The Instructors Guide to Anthropology.* CRM Books. 1971.

Chapter 4

Breay, Clare. Harrison, Julian. "Magna Carta, An Introduction," July 28, 2014.

Bacon, F., 1620. *The New Organon (Novum Organum),* ed. by Lisa Jardine and Michael Silverthorne, Cambridge: Cambridge University Press, 2000.

Bristow, William. "Enlightenment," November 2017. https://plato.stanford.edu/entries/enlightenment/

Jean Jacques Rousseau, *The Social Contract.* Internet Encylopedia of Philosophy.

Levin, David. *The Puritans in the Enlightenment.* Rand McNally. 1963.

Locke, John. *The Second Treatise of Government.* the Bobbs. Merrill Company Inc. 1952

Chapter 5

Fedar Bernard. *The Process of American Government.* Nobel & Nobel. 1972.

Hirschfield, Robert S. *The Constitution, and the Court.* Random House, Inc. 1962.

Quotes From the Convention. 1787.

Chapter 6

Curti, Merle. *The Growth of American Thought.* Harper & Brothers. 1943.

Quotes From the Convention. 1787.

Chapter 7

Curti, Merle. *The Growth of American Thought.* Harper & Brothers. 1943.

Quotes From the Convention. 1787.

Chapter 8

Bishop, Hillmand. M Hendel, Samuel. *The Basic Issues of American Democracy.* 1948.

Fishel Jr., Leslie H, Quarles, Benjamin. *The Black American.* Scott Foresman & Company. 1967

Chapter 9

"Heroine Of The Revolutionary War," History of American Women.

"Mary Murray," American Revolutionary War Talk.

Chapter 10

Curti, Merle. *The Growth of American Thought.* Harper & Brothers. 1943.

Bishop, Hillmand. M Hendel, Samuel. *The Basic Issues of American Democracy.* 1948.

Chapter 11

Adams, Henry. *The Unite, States in 1800.* Cornell University Press. 1955.

"The life of Sally Hemings," October 2017, https://www.monticello.org/sally-hemings/

Koch, Adrienne. *Jefferson & Ma,ison.* Oxford University Press. 1964.

Padover, Saul, K. *Thomas Jefferson on Democracy.* New American Library. 1939.

Pancake, John S. *Thomas Jefferson & Alexan,er Hamilton.* Barrons Educational series. 1974.

Chapter 12

"African Americans and the War of 1812," National Parks Service.

Essays: Second Series, James Munroe (Boston, MA), 1844.

Jensen, Merrill. 1905. *The New Nation: A History of the Unite* States During the Confe*eration 1781-1789*

"Jackson's Message to Congress," National Archives.

Schlesinger, Arthur M. *The Age of Jackson.* Mentor Books. 1949.

Chapter 13

"Bleeding Kansas," History.com Editors. April 7, 2021.

Chapter 14

"President Lincoln," Whitehouse.com.

"Abraham Lincoln," Battlefields.org.

Chapter 15

"Mary Wollstonecraft on Motherhood and Political Participation: An Overlooked Insight into Women's Subordination," January 2020.

Kerri Lee Alexander, NWHM Fellow, 2018. "Sarah Moore Grimke,"

"Susan B Anthony," Women's Rights. Crusade for the Vote.

"Elizabeth C Stanton," Women's History.

"Lucy Stone," Women's Rights.

"Harriot Tubman," Women's History.

"Harriot Beacher Stow," National Women's History Museum.

Chapter 16

Whittier, John Greenleaf. 1892. *The Poetical Works in Four Volumes.* "The Farewell of a Virginia Slave Mother" Chapter 17

"Civil Rights and Truman," National Park Service.

"The Marshal Plan," Truman Library, 2022.

Chapter 18

Turner, Henry, A. *Politics in the Unite, States.* McGraw-Hill Book Company. 1955.

Summary

Mercieca, Jennifer. Rangappa, Asha. "The Ancient Greeks' Guide To Rejecting Propaganda and Disinformation," June 7, 2020.

Bibliography

Adams, H. (1955). *The Unite States in 1800.* Cornell University Press.

American Battlefield Trust. (2022). *Two Wars for Inepenence: The Revolution an War of 1812.* https://www.battlefields.org/learn/articles/two-wars-independence.

Averett, Ginny A. October 30, 2004. *The unsung hero of the revolutionary war.* Excellent-ebooks.Com/ Bucky

Beals, Ralph, & Hijer, H . (1959). *An Introuction to Anthropology.* The Macmillan Company.

Berreman, G. et al. (1971) *Anthropology Today.* CRM Bools.

Bill of Rights Institute. (2022). Webster-Hayne Debates, 1830.

Bishop, H. &. Hendel, S. M. (1948). *The Basic Issues of American Democracy.*

Brogan, D.W. (1944). *The American Character.* Alfred A Knob.

Burns, J., Peltason, J. W. (1952). *Government by the People.* Presnite Hall Inc.

Calhoun, D. et al. (1957). *An Introuction to Social Science.* JB. Lippincott Company.

Colton, B. (1958). *Book of the Revolution.* American Heritage Publishing Company.

Curti, M. (1943). *The Growth of American Thought.* Harper & Brothers.

Davis, K. (1948). *Human Society,* The MacMillan Company.

Ebenstein, W. (1951). *Great Political Thinkers.* Rinehart & Company.

Elliott, W. (1949). *Western Political Heritage.* Prentice-Hall Inc.

Ellis, J. S. (2000). *Foun ation Brothers.* Vintage Books..

Fedar B. (1972). *The Process of American Government.* Nobel & Nobel.

Fishel Jr., L. H., & Quarles, B. (1967). *The Black American.* Scott Foresman & Company.

Foster, K., French, D., Stanley, J. & Chatterton Williams, T. (2021, July 6). The Misguided Bans on Critical Race Theory. *New York Times.*

Grimes, A. P. (1955). *American Political Thought.* Holt, Rinehart & Winston Inc.

Hayes, C. Jr. (1939). *A Political Cultural History of Mo esan Europe.* Volume H, MacMillan Company.

Hirschfield, R. S. (1962). *The Constitution an the Court.* Random House, Inc.

History.com. (2022). Abigail Adams urges husband to "remember the ladies" https://www.history.com/this-day-in-history/abigail-adams-urges-husband-to-remember-the-ladies.

Kluckhorn, C. de. (1949). *Mirror For Man.* McGraw Hill Book Company Inc.

Kock, A. (1961). *Power, Morals, an the Foun ing Fathers.* Cornell University Press.

Koch, A. (1964). *Jefferson & Ma ison.* Oxford University Press.

Kollenberg, B. (1961). *Origin of the American Revolution 1759-1766.* Collier Books.

Krauthammer, B. "Slavery," *The Encyclope ia of Oklahoma History an Culture,* https://www.okhistory.org/publications/enc/entry.php?entry=SL003.

Locke, J. (1952). *The Secon Treatise of Government.* the Bobbs. Merrill Company Inc.

Levin, D. (1963). *The Puritan in the Enlightenment.* Rand McNally.

Meier, A. (2020, June 7). *'Say their names': Stories of Black Americans kille by police.* ABC7NY.com.

Magic, R. F. *(1953). Rebels vs. Royalists.* Scholastic Book Servies.

McCullough, D. (2001). *John A ams.* Simon & Shuster.

NYSED.gov. (2019). *About the New York State E*▪*ucation Department.*

Padover, S. K. (1939). *Thomas Jefferson on Democracy.* New American Library.

Pancake, J. S. (1974). *Thomas Jefferson & Alexan*▪*er Hamilton.* Barrons Educational series.

Plato. (1991). *The Republic.* Vintage Books.

Riser-Kositsky, M. (2019, Jan 3). Education Statistics: Facts About American Schools. Education Week.

Rosenbaum, H. D. (1972). *A First Book in Politics & Government.* The Dryden Press.

Ross, G. (1993). *Dave.* Warner Brothers Pictures.

Schlesinger, A. M. (1949). *The Age of Jackson.* Mentor Books.

Sorkin, A. (1995). The American President. Universal Pictures.

Staples, B. (2022, Aug. 10). American Joined the Cult of the Confederacy. New York Times.

Swartz, M. (1971). *The Instructors Gui*▪*e to Anthropology.* CRM Books.

Szalai, J. (2021, Aug. 31). When Frederick Douglass met Andrew Johnson. *New York Times.*

Traub, J. (2022, April 10.) Everyman as President. *New York Times.*

Turner, H. A. (1955). *Politics in the Unite*▪ *States.* McGraw-Hill Book Company.

Tyson, N. D. (2020, June 3). Reflections on the Color of My Skin. https://www.haydenplanetarium.org/tyson/commentary/2020-06-03-reflections-on-color-of-my-skin.php.

Zinn, C. J. (1959). *How our Laws are Ma*▪*e.* United States Government Printing Office.

Made in the USA
Middletown, DE
18 September 2022